EAT LIKE
A MONK

EAT LIKE A MONK

A Plant-Based Guide to Conscious Cooking and Mindful Eating

JODY EDDY

NewSeed
PRESS

CONTENTS

INTRODUCTION

The journey through the realm of monastic temple cuisine—a tradition deeply rooted in Buddhist monasteries throughout Asia and other parts of the world—is an uplifting and transformative one. In this book, you will embark upon an exploration of the profound connection between food, mindfulness, gratitude, and well-being. Drawing inspiration from the principles of transference and conscious living, this book invites you to discover the life-changing power of mindful eating that monks have embraced for centuries.

Monastic temple cuisine transcends the act of mere sustenance. It is an ancient practice centered on consciously growing food, cooking it, and consuming it—a holistic approach that reflects the essence of attentiveness that defines this culinary philosophy. By immersing ourselves in monastic traditions, we learn to infuse intention into every aspect of our culinary rituals, from the cultivation of sustainably grown and harvested ingredients to the final presentation and enjoyment of each recipe.

At the heart of monastic temple cuisine lies the belief that the quality of the food we consume is influenced by the intentions behind its growth and preparation. When food is cultivated and cooked with consciousness and the intent of offering it to a deity—and when our recipes do not contain ingredients that harmed other living beings—it undergoes a remarkable transformation. The resulting dish becomes a reflection of the devotion and care put into its creation—it becomes lighter, brighter, and carries a spiritual essence that can uplift the mind and nourish the soul. Conversely, if negative emotions like anger, disregard for life, sorrow, or jealousy taint the cooking process, these emotions can find their way into the food, subtly affecting those who partake in its consumption.

Within the pages of this book, you will be immersed in the notion of transference—the idea that the energy and intentions invested in our food can directly impact our well-being. Through modern research, supported by science to back up this ancient belief system and timeless wisdom, you will explore the interconnectedness of intention and food, witnessing the profound influence that conscious growing, cooking, and hospitality can have on the final outcome of our meals.

Monastic temple cuisine opens the door to cultivating a state of deep and enriching mindfulness when it comes to nourishing our bodies, our spirits, and one another. It encourages us to approach meals as a form of meditation, where we engage all our senses and are fully present in the empowering act of eating. Mindful eating goes beyond the physical act of consumption—it entails savoring each bite; appreciating the flavors,

colors, textures, and nourishment that our food provides; and honoring the journey the ingredients undertook to reach our plates. By embracing this practice, we can develop a deeper connection with the sustenance we receive, fostering gratitude, grace, and a sense of unity with the world around us.

Vegetarianism, veganism, and plant-based diets form an integral part of monastic temple cuisine. This tradition recognizes the ethical, health, and environmental benefits of these dietary choices, celebrating the abundance of flavors and ingredients that nature provides. In this book, you will find a collection of vegan and vegetarian recipes inspired by monastic temple cuisine—a testament to the richness, diversity, compassion, and deliciousness rooted in plant-based cooking.

While monastic temple cuisine carries with it the enigmatic stirring of ancient wisdom, it remains relevant and adaptable to our modern world. As you navigate the challenges and stresses of contemporary life, the practice of cooking and eating like a monk can bring moments of tranquility, rejuvenation, and solidarity with the people you love. It offers you an opportunity to slow down, reconnect with the present moment, and cultivate a deeper appreciation for the planet that sustains all life.

Through this book, you will be gently guided along a pathway of incorporating the principles of monastic temple cuisine into your daily life in a simple and manageable way. The pages are filled with practical suggestions on how to infuse mindfulness into your meal preparation, embrace the art of mindful

eating, and create a harmonious relationship with the food you consume. You are invited to explore the possibilities of incorporating monastic temple cuisine into your own culinary repertoire, encouraging a more intentional and nourishing way of life.

As you journey through the culinary traditions of monastic temple cuisine, you will uncover not only its profound impact on your personal well-being but also its contribution to a healthier planet. With a conscious approach to growing, cooking, and eating, we align ourselves with sustainable practices that prioritize our bodily health and that of the environment we inhabit.

This is a culinary odyssey in which food becomes a meditation and each meal becomes an opportunity for transcendence, and where balance, rituals, routines, seasonality, sustainability, simplicity, and gratitude are celebrated. By embracing conscious growing, cooking, and eating, we can elevate the act of nourishment into a transformative experience. Prepare to awaken your senses, nurture your body, and discover the profound connection between food and mindful living by immersing yourself in the world of monastic temple cuisine.

By embracing this perspective, we can experience profound healing—for our bodies, our minds, our spirits, other living beings, and our magnificent planet that works so hard for us. Mindful eating nurtures our physical well-being, as we learn to listen to our bodies and provide them with the nourishment they need. It fosters mental clarity and emotional balance, allowing us to develop a harmonious relationship with food and the world around us. By adopting plant-based diets and sustainable practices, we contribute to the healing of the earth, recognizing our interconnectedness with the environment and taking actionable steps toward a more sustainable future.

This kind of mindful eating has the power to awaken a sense of joy, empowerment, resiliency, peacefulness, and fulfillment within us. When we learn to eat like a monk, we become more attuned to our needs and desires, leading to a greater sense of self-awareness and self-care. We discover the pleasure and satisfaction that comes from savoring each bite, cultivating gratitude for the nourishment we receive.

It is not only Buddhist monks who embraced this way of eating. There is a line from the Sikh spiritual text Guru Granth Sahib that says, "The body is the field of action . . . as you plant, so shall you harvest." This sentiment echoes the teachings of various spiritual traditions that emphasize the importance of mindful consumption. Sikhism in particular teaches that food should be treated with respect and gratitude, and that by eating mindfully, we honor the divine presence within us, and one another.

Even Catholic monastics have recognized the significance of mindful eating. Saint Benedict, the father of Western monasticism, spoke of the importance of moderation and mindfulness in meals. He advised his followers to eat and drink in a manner that nurtures both the body and the soul, understanding that the act of eating can be a spiritual practice when approached with intention and gratitude.

"Breathe in deeply to bring your mind home to your body." These words, spoken by the renowned Buddhist monk Thich Nhat Hanh, resonate deeply in the realm of mindful eating. Thich Nhat Hanh emphasized the importance of bringing our full presence and awareness to the act of eating, recognizing that it is not just a physical necessity but an opportunity for spiritual nourishment. He speaks of the transference of energy and intention from the food to the one who consumes it, highlighting the transformative power of mindful eating.

This practice extends beyond our individual experiences—it has the potential to improve our relationships, our daily lives, our resplendent planet, and our future. As we embrace the tenets of eating like a monk, we deepen our connections with others, fostering a sense of togetherness and shared experiences around the table. By incorporating the principles of monastic temple cuisine into our daily lives, we become conscious participants in shaping a healthier, more mindful society.

Through this culinary journey, you are invited to explore the transformative power of mindful eating, to embark on a path of self-discovery, and to create a positive impact on both your own well-being and the world around you. Get ready to savor the flavors, embrace the present moment, and embark on an extraordinary adventure of nourishment, illumination, and enlightenment. You are invited to begin your exploration of monastic temple cuisine, where food becomes a gateway to joy, empowerment, and a brighter future.

A NOTE ON THE RECIPES

Temple cuisine is a remarkable culinary tradition steeped in the enduring philosophy of ahimsa, non-harm, an ethos that extends beyond our interactions with others to our relationship with food and the environment. This cookbook endeavors to guide you through a plant-based culinary journey that respects this philosophy. It introduces you to a world where meals are prepared with an attitude of reverence, where the divine is seen in every ingredient, and where there is a deep gratitude for the life that sustains us.

Each recipe within these pages tells a tale, embodying lessons of compassion, coexistence, respect for our environment and one another, and the prioritization of conservation that are intrinsic to Buddhist and other monastic teachings. These are dishes that are as benevolent as they are delectable, proving that the path to culinary satisfaction need not cause harm to any living being.

The practices are drawn from temple kitchens scattered throughout Asia, each of them contributing their unique flavors, techniques, and ancient wisdom to a vast, shared culinary tapestry. These ancient temple kitchens have long been places of innovation, their recipes an artful blend of the spiritual and the sensory. There is an inherent respect for the natural rhythms of nature, a preference for seasonal and local ingredients, and a mindful approach to minimizing waste.

In adhering to a plant-based diet, monastic cuisine does more than just abstain from animal products. It also advocates for a gentler, more sustainable way of living and eating. Every meal is an exercise in conscious cooking and consumption, encouraging us to consider the impacts of our food choices on our body, mind, and environment.

What awaits you in the following pages is more than just a collection of recipes. It's a gateway to a time-honored culinary practice that satiates not just the palate but also the soul. Every dish you prepare and partake in is an opportunity to express gratitude, connect with your food, and make your mealtime a meditative ritual.

Through this book, the hope is to demystify these distinct culinary traditions, to demonstrate how approachable they are, and inspire you to explore and incorporate elements of monastic cooking into your own kitchen routines. Here is your chance to transform beloved dishes into healthier, more sustainable versions without losing their essence. Let this be an invitation to embark on a journey of flavors that brings the ancient wisdom of monastic cuisine to your modern kitchen, one meal at a time.

OVERALL PHILOSOPHY

AND TECHNIQUES THAT SUPPORT IT

The essence of monastic cuisine goes beyond *what's* being prepared; it's also about *how* it's prepared. In these kitchens, every ingredient is handled with reverence, and there's a deep appreciation for the sustenance it provides. For instance, vegetables like carrots and potatoes are often left unpeeled, while greens are preserved to maximize their nutritional value and minimize food waste. No part of the food is discarded, with often-overlooked parts like cauliflower leaves, beet greens, and carrot tops used creatively to provide unique flavors and textures.

Monastic philosophy emphasizes respect for all forms of life, and this extends to minimizing waste and embracing recycling. Leftovers are either repurposed or composted, aligning with the concept of zero waste. Conscious eating is practiced, which means cooking only what will be consumed to eliminate food waste.

In monastic kitchens, steaming is a frequently used cooking method, as it preserves the natural flavors and nutrients of the food. Bamboo steamers are essential tools for this purpose. Stir-frying is another common technique, emphasizing high heat to retain vibrant colors and crisp textures in vegetables.

To promote a balanced diet and overall health, lower-sodium alternatives to saltier items like soy sauce are recommended. In traditional recipes, sweeteners like jaggery or palm sugar are often used, but these ingredients can harm ecosystems. In accordance with the monastic principle of non-harm, these sweeteners are substituted with more benevolent options like agave and maple syrup, with dark brown sugar and granulated sugar used when necessary. Many monastic recipes are traditionally served with rice. Opt for brown rice when possible, as it is healthier than white rice. Serving food in warm bowls enhances the comforting and soothing dining experience.

The recipes in this book are free of animal products like eggs and dairy. However, if a dairy product could enhance a dish, it is recommended to use a plant-based alternative.

Monks cook in harmony with the seasons, adapting to locally available produce. You're encouraged to do the same—be creative, flexible, and responsive to seasonal and local ingredients. This approach not only enhances flavor but also supports local farmers and food producers while enriching your heart and spirit.

As for kitchen tools, a bamboo mat for rolling dishes like kimbap, a bamboo steamer for healthy steaming, and a versatile wok for stir-frying, deep-frying, and even steaming are essential items. These tools introduce you to a world where meals are prepared with an attitude of reverence, where the divine is seen in every ingredient, and where there is a deep gratitude for the life that sustains us.

INGREDIENTS

Most of these ingredients can be found in popular supermarket chains, but some might be more easily sourced from Asian specialty markets. Substitution suggestions are provided where appropriate. This journey into monastic temple cuisine encourages flexibility, creativity, and respect for food—principles you will hopefully carry beyond the confines of these recipes into your everyday life. Here are ingredients that might be more unusual.

Banana Leaves: Used widely in Asian cooking for wrapping food before steaming or grilling, banana leaves lend a distinct, aromatic flavor and also serve as natural, biodegradable food wrappers.

Besan: Besan, also known as gram flour or chickpea flour, is a type of flour made from ground chickpeas. It's common in Indian, Pakistani, Bangladeshi, and other South Asian cuisines, where it's enjoyed in a variety of dishes, such as pakoras (a type of fritter) and laddus (a sweet treat), and in batter for certain types of fried foods. It's naturally gluten-free, is high in protein, and has a slightly nutty flavor. It's also used in some beauty and skin care routines, as it's thought to have skin cleansing and brightening properties. Besan is widely available at Asian specialty markets.

Danmuji: Korean yellow pickled radish, known for its crisp texture and tangy-sweet flavor, danmuji is used in kimbap and often served alongside other Korean dishes as a palate cleanser.

Dashi: This simple broth forms the base of many Japanese dishes. Made from kombu (dried kelp) and bonito fish flakes, it's known for its umami depth (see page 105), although vegan versions can be made just from kelp.

Dehydrated Lotus Seeds: Also known as makhana in India, these seeds have a sweet, nutty flavor and are often used in desserts or puffed for snacks.

Eno: Also known as fruit salt, eno is a quick-acting antacid comprising sodium bicarbonate, citric acid, and sodium carbonate, which are key effervescence-producing ingredients. It plays a vital role in dhokla, a popular Indian dish, by aiding in its fermentation, making the snack fluffy and light.

Galangal: A rhizome related to ginger, with sharper, more citrusy notes, galangal is used in many Southeast Asian curries and soups, and it's prized for its ability to add complex flavor profiles.

Jackfruit: This large tropical fruit has a fibrous texture that, when cooked, can mimic pulled pork or shredded chicken, making it a popular meat substitute in vegan and vegetarian dishes.

Makrut Lime Leaves: The leaves of the makrut lime tree are often used in Southeast Asian cuisine. They impart a strong, floral citrus aroma and flavor to dishes, especially curries and soups.

Kelp: A type of large brown seaweed that grows in underwater forests, kelp is often dried and used to make broths, as it imparts a subtle brininess and umami flavor.

Khao Khua: Thai roasted rice powder, made by toasting glutinous rice until golden and grinding it finely, imparts a nutty flavor and texture to dishes, especially salads like larb.

Mirin: This sweet Japanese rice wine is used to add subtle sweetness to marinades, glazes, and sauces as well as to balance salty flavors in dishes.

Miso: A Japanese staple made from fermented soybeans mixed with salt and a type of fungus called koji, miso paste is versatile, adding depth and richness to soups, marinades, and dressings. Its umami character makes it an integral part of many Asian dishes.

Nori: A type of seaweed that's dried and pressed into thin sheets, nori is used widely in Japanese cuisine, especially for wrapping sushi and onigiri (rice balls).

Rice Vinegar: Made from fermented rice, rice vinegar has a mild, sweetly tart flavor. It's a key ingredient in sushi rice and also used in marinades, pickles, and salad dressings.

Sakura Extract: Derived from cherry blossoms (sakura in Japanese), this extract is used as a delicate, floral sweetener in pastries, teas, and some savory dishes.

Seitan: Also known as "wheat meat," seitan is made from gluten, the main protein of wheat. With its meat-like texture, it's a favorite in stir-fries, stews, and grilled dishes.

Spring Roll Wrappers and Dumpling Wrappers: These thin sheets of dough are essential in Asian cuisine. Spring roll wrappers are used for wrapping fillings like vegetables and tofu for spring rolls, while dumpling wrappers encase fillings for dumplings, which are then steamed, boiled, or pan-fried.

Tamari: A Japanese soy sauce made mainly from soybeans with little to no wheat, tamari is a popular choice for those seeking a gluten-free alternative. It has a darker color and richer flavor than traditional soy sauce.

Tamarind Concentrate: Derived from the tamarind fruit, the concentrate provides a sweet-sour taste that's essential in many Indian, Thai, and Mexican dishes.

Tempeh: Originating from Indonesia, this fermented soybean product is known for its firm texture and nutty flavor. It absorbs marinades well and can be used in stir-fries, salads, and sandwiches as a protein source.

Tofu: Tofu is made from curdled fresh soy milk, which is pressed into solid blocks. Its mild flavor makes it a versatile ingredient in everything from savory mains to sweet desserts.

Umeboshi: These pickled plums from Japan are known for their unique salty, sour, and slightly sweet flavor. They're often served with rice or used as a flavoring in sauces and vinaigrettes.

Vegan Fish Sauce: Created from fermented soybeans and mushrooms, vegan fish sauce imitates the savory, umami taste found in traditional fish sauce. Used as a seasoning in numerous dishes, it can heighten flavor profiles without using any animal products.

ASCETICISM & MODERATION

At the heart of the ancient tradition of monastic temple cuisine lies the practice of asceticism and moderation, guiding the lives of monks and influencing every aspect of their food cultivation, preparation, and consumption. In this chapter, we explore the sacred principles that have sustained Asian temples for centuries to inspire us to lead more mindful and fulfilling lives.

Buddhist monks in particular exemplify simplicity in their food preparation, embracing humble ingredients to create meaningful and nourishing meals. They eschew indulgent extravagances in their ingredients and cooking techniques to focus on the essence of sustenance—a reflection of their detachment from material desires. Through limited food choices, monks find contentment and liberation from the distractions of desire, preference, and attachment. Within each monastic dining experience, contemplative eating becomes a spiritual practice—a brilliant moment of reflection and gratitude. As they savor each bite, the monks are fully present, cultivating a deeper connection with the nourishment their bodies and minds receive.

Fasting is a familiar ritual at monastic temples; it is a customary practice, especially during religious observances. This restraint serves as a purification process, honing the self-discipline essential for spiritual growth and reducing attachment to the mere pleasure of eating. The profound act of alms, where monks humbly walk through the community, relying on the generosity of others for their daily sustenance, fosters a sense of interdependence and promotes humility within the monastic lifestyle.

Not wasting food and the avoidance of luxurious ingredients are also vital aspects of monastic temple cuisine. Leftovers are honored, reflecting the respect monks have for the effort and resources that went into producing the food. By refraining from excess, monks align themselves with the essence of simplicity and embrace the notion that consuming only what is necessary supports their spiritual practice and, ultimately, their well-being.

A renowned Buddhist monk, Bhikkhu Bodhi, once eloquently expressed the significance of moderation and asceticism in food preparation and consumption in the Pali Canon (also known as the Tipitaka, scriptures from the Theravada Buddhist tradition), stating, "The training in renunciation and the refusal to accept gifts of special food arise from the same principle: to free the mind from bondage to the taste of food." These principles encapsulate the core essence of monastic temple cuisine, providing a road map for cultivating mindfulness, detachment, and spiritual growth.

Beyond the walls of the monastery, the lessons of asceticism and moderation have profound relevance for the modern person. In a world often characterized by excess and overindulgence, incorporating these teachings into our daily lives can lead to transformative benefits. By embracing simplicity in food preparation, we can discover the joy of nourishment in its purest form and cultivate an appreciation for the inherent value of basic ingredients.

Science also lends support to the principles of asceticism and moderation in food growing, preparation, and consumption. Research shows that excessive food intake, particularly of processed and unhealthy foods, is linked to various health issues, including obesity, heart disease, and diabetes. Adopting a more moderate and mindful approach to eating can improve overall health and well-being.

Embracing moderation and asceticism can help us develop self-discipline and self-awareness, empowering us to make conscious and meaningful decisions in all aspects of life.

…하여 나쁜 친구를 사귀지 않고,

…라. 어른을 공경하고, 덕 있는 이…

…고, 모르는 이를 너그럽게 용서하라…

…는 것을 잡지 말고, 내 몸 대우 없음…

…음에 원망하지 말라.

…이 자기에게 돌아오고,

…재화가 따르느니라.

Stir-Fried Shiitake Mushrooms with Ginger

SERVES 4

Shiitake mushrooms are a favorite ingredient in Zen Buddhist cooking because they offer the savory umami flavor that is so beloved in Japanese cuisine. Ginger and rice vinegar brighten the shiitake's earthy flavor while a splash of soy sauce intensifies the umami. Stir-frying is a common technique in Japanese temple cuisine because it's an unfussy method embodying the simplicity of Zen cooking while coaxing out the full flavor potential of the ingredients.

---

1 lb (450 g) shiitake mushrooms, stems removed and saved for another use

1 tablespoon vegetable oil

1 teaspoon minced, peeled fresh ginger

1 tablespoon soy sauce

2 teaspoons rice vinegar

Cooked rice for serving (optional)

Remove excess residue from the shiitake tops by gently rubbing them with a damp kitchen cloth. Avoid oversaturating the mushrooms because they are like sponges and will absorb the excess liquid. Using a sharp paring knife, score the tops of the shiitakes to enable them to release and absorb liquid more uniformly. Slice the tops into halves or quarters, depending upon their size.

Heat the oil in a wok or a pan over medium heat. Reduce the heat to medium-low. Add the shiitakes and ginger and stir-fry until the shiitakes have released most of their liquid and are tender, about 7 minutes. Add the soy sauce and rice vinegar and stir-fry until the shiitakes have absorbed about half of the liquid and are glistening, about 2 minutes.

Serve as a side dish or with rice for a complete meal. Store in a covered container in the refrigerator for up to 2 days.

Mock Meats in Monastic Plant-Based Cooking

A monastic lifestyle typically encompasses a commitment to compassion, extending to all living beings. This path naturally leads many monks to a plant-based way of living, with mock meats playing a crucial role in maintaining traditional flavors and textures in their culinary practices while also adding an essential source of protein. Through the use of mock meats, monastic cooking honors the Buddhist principles of compassion and non-harm, ensuring that every meal is a conscious step along the path of empathy and kindness.

Within Buddhist cuisines, especially in East Asian monasteries, the art of creating mock meats (inspired by their traditional counterparts) from soy, gluten, fruit, and mushrooms has been perfected over centuries, enabling monks to adhere to vegetarian diets without compromising texture, nutrition, flavor, or culinary traditions. Here's a glimpse into various mock meats and their significance in Buddhist monastic cooking.

Tofu
Made from soybeans, tofu is an extremely versatile ingredient, adaptable to various cooking methods and capable of absorbing diverse flavors. It is a staple in monastic kitchens, used in myriad dishes.

Tempeh
Tempeh, another soy-based product, has a nutty flavor and a firm texture that holds up well during the cooking process. Its fermented nature not only adds depth of flavor to dishes but also aligns with healthful eating.

Seitan
Created from wheat gluten, seitan possesses a chewy, meat-like texture and is rich in protein. In monastic cooking, it serves as an important ingredient in various preparations.

Textured Vegetable Protein (TVP)
As a dehydrated soy product, TVP transforms upon rehydration, closely mimicking the texture of ground meat. It is integrated into traditional temple dishes to add protein, variety, and substance.

Mock Duck
Created from wheat gluten, mock duck provides a firm texture and a savory component to stir-fries, curries, and stews.

Soy Protein Mock Meats
These take on various forms, emulating chicken, beef, or seafood, and are incorporated into traditional dishes re-envisioned for a monastic plant-based diet.

Shiitake Mushrooms
Prized for their deep umami flavor, shiitake mushrooms contribute a meaty dimension to soups, stews, and stir-fries.

Jackfruit
In its young, unripe state, jackfruit offers a texture reminiscent of meat, becoming a compassionate substitute in dishes like stir-fries, salads, and soups.

Vegetarian Noodle Soup

SERVES 4

Phở is an iconic noodle soup in Vietnam that typically features beef or chicken. It's a popular menu item at Vietnamese temples where a vegetarian version, referred to as phở chay, is typically served. For this recipe, the traditionally meat-based broth is replaced with a rich, flavorful vegetable broth, and tofu is used as the main protein source. The soup also includes traditional phở noodles (rice noodles) that are garnished with bean sprouts, lime wedges, and fresh cilantro. Cinnamon and star anise are added to the broth to offer the depth of flavor that onions, garlic, and ginger would traditionally impart.

1 block (8 oz/225 g) extra-firm tofu

2 tablespoons vegetable oil

3 qt (2.7 L) low-sodium vegetable broth

1 star anise pod

1 cinnamon stick

1 package (8 oz/225 g) phở noodles

1 red chile, thinly sliced (optional)

2 oz (56 g) bean sprouts

⅓ cup (10 g) loosely packed fresh cilantro leaves

1 lime, cut into quarters

Place the tofu on a dry kitchen towel, wrap it up, and press out as much liquid as possible. Slice the tofu into triangles or squares, depending upon your preference. Heat the oil in a pan over medium heat. Add the tofu and fry until golden brown, about 3 minutes, flipping once during the frying process to ensure even cooking. Transfer to a plate lined with paper towels to drain.

Add the vegetable broth, star anise, and cinnamon stick to a pot and bring to a boil over high heat. Reduce the heat to medium-low and simmer gently for 15 minutes to infuse the broth with the spices. Remove the spices using a slotted spoon and add the noodles to the broth. Raise the heat to medium and cook until the noodles are tender, about 7 minutes.

To serve, distribute the noodles among 4 warm bowls. Pour the broth over the noodles and top it with the fried tofu cubes, sliced chiles, bean sprouts, and cilantro. Serve with lime wedges on the side. The phở will keep in a covered container in the refrigerator for up to 2 days.

Avoiding Foods with Strong Flavors and Odors

Buddhist philosophy, deeply rooted in principles of moderation and non-harming, extends to the dietary practices of its monks. Within this tradition, foods with strong odors or flavors, like garlic, chiles, and onions, are typically avoided. The reason lies in the teachings of the Buddha and the concept of the Middle Way (see page 60).

The Buddha advised his followers to refrain from consuming certain foods, such as those with pungent flavors, as they were believed to stimulate the senses excessively, possibly leading to an imbalance in the mind and body. The objective was to maintain a sense of calm and clarity, enabling better focus during meditation and encouraging detachment from worldly desires and distractions.

Buddhist monks often follow Vinaya Pitaka, one of the three main Tripitaka (Buddhist scriptures), which contains rules for monastic discipline, including food. Some of these rules about food, however, can vary among different Buddhist sects and cultures.

Specifically, garlic and onions are considered to be aphrodisiacs, stimulants, or sleep-inducing agents, disrupting the equilibrium and tranquility that is desired in monastic life. These ingredients are therefore omitted from monastic temple cuisine (and many of the recipes in this book) to promote mental and physical moderation.

These ingredients are also avoided due to their strong odors. In the communal living environment of a monastery, strong-smelling foods might disturb other practitioners, infringing upon the principle of non-harm or not causing discomfort to others.

At its essence, the dietary practices of Buddhist monks exemplify their holistic approach to spiritual development and mindfulness, manifesting through conscious, considerate consumption and respect for others.

FAN TUAN

TAIWAN

Rice Balls

SERVES 4

Fan tuan are rice balls that offer the monks at Taiwanese Buddhist temples a nutritional boost that aligns with their adherence to moderation, while also providing them with a pleasurable dining experience, since they are fun to eat. Think of the sushi rice as a blank canvas for your fan tuan. Here they are prepared three different ways, using red beet juice, matcha, and white sesame paste, which is readily available at Asian specialty markets.

3 cups (465 g) cooked sushi rice, prepared according to the package instructions

2 tablespoons red beet juice (preferably freshly squeezed)

1 tablespoon matcha powder

3 tablespoons warm water

2 tablespoons white sesame paste

⅔ cup (75 g) finely shredded carrot

⅔ cup (60 g) finely sliced baby bok choy (green and white parts)

1 tablespoon low-sodium soy sauce

1 teaspoon white sesame seeds

1 teaspoon black sesame seeds

For the beet fan tuan, gently stir together 1 cup (155 g) of the rice and the beet juice until the rice is evenly coated. For the matcha fan tuan, dissolve the matcha in 2 tablespoons of the warm water and then mix with 1 cup (155 g) of the rice until the rice is evenly coated. For the white sesame fan tuan, stir together the white sesame paste with the remaining 1 tablespoon of warm water and then mix with the remaining 1 cup (155 g) of rice until it is evenly coated.

Add one-third of the carrot, bok choy, soy sauce, white sesame seeds, and black sesame seeds to each rice variety and gently stir each together until the ingredients are incorporated. Roll the fan tuan into 1- to 2-inch (2.5- to 5-cm) balls, depending upon your size preference. Serve right away. The fan tuan will keep in a covered container in the refrigerator for up to 2 days.

ZHI MA JIANG HUANG GUA

CHINA

Lightly Pickled Sesame Cucumbers

SERVES 4

These lightly pickled cucumbers reflect the principles of moderation that Buddhist monks typically adhere to in that the flavors are not overpowering and the pickling process is simple and fast. These refreshing pickles frequently accompany meals at Buddhist temples in China, where they are appreciated for their bright and tangy flavor and crunchy texture.

2 cucumbers

1 tablespoon low–sodium soy sauce

1 tablespoon rice vinegar

1 tablespoon toasted sesame oil

1 teaspoon brown sugar

½ teaspoon salt

Red pepper flakes (optional)

Sesame seeds, for garnish

Cut the ends off of each cucumber. Quarter each cucumber lengthwise and then cut each of these pieces in half horizontally (repeat the process once more if you prefer smaller pickles). In a large bowl, combine the soy sauce, rice vinegar, sesame oil, brown sugar, salt, and red pepper flakes to taste, if using. Whisk until the sugar is dissolved. Add the cucumbers and stir gently until they are well coated. Sprinkle with sesame seeds. Transfer to a covered container and refrigerate for at least 30 minutes but up to 2 days before serving. Serve with other dishes or enjoy on their own as a crunchy snack.

Jingwansa Temple
South Korea

Nestled within the serene mountains of Eunpyeong-gu, South Korea, the historic Jingwansa Temple is renowned for its rich heritage of monastic cuisine. Celebrated for its vegetarian offerings, the temple food is a mindful practice of asceticism and moderation, reflecting the lifestyle of the resident monks. Unfussy yet diverse, the dishes include delicately steamed lotus root, the subtle yet flavorful sanchae bibimbap, a medley of wild mountain vegetables and gently grilled dishes wrapped in perilla leaves.

The temple complex, a time capsule of Korean Buddhist architecture, conveys an aura of tranquility, with its elegantly understated wooden structures embraced by lush greenery. Notable among them, the main hall dates back to the 17th century CE, making it a significant historical landmark.

Over the decades, Jingwansa Temple has become a pilgrimage site for culinary and spiritual enthusiasts. Visitors can taste the same temple dishes enjoyed by the monks, providing a flavorful glimpse into their daily rituals and a snapshot into monastic life. Guided by principles of balance and humility, the preparation of temple food at Jingwansa Temple is a meditative practice that respects nature's seasons and cycles, fosters a deeper understanding of Korean Buddhist culture, and offers an enlightening experience that transcends the simple act of eating.

Bean Sprout Salad

SERVES 8

Banchan are small side dishes that are typically served alongside rice in Korean monastic cuisine. They are an important component of the meal not only for the synergy of colors, textures, and flavors they offer but also because banchan provides a variety of nutritional benefits for the monks. One of the most iconic Korean banchan is kimchi. Kongnamul muchim is a traditional banchan that is a staple at nearly every monastic temple meal in Korea. It's a simply prepared bean sprout salad that aligns with a Korean monk's commitment to moderation.

1 teaspoon minced, peeled fresh ginger

1 tablespoon vegan fish sauce

2 teaspoons soy sauce

2 teaspoons toasted sesame oil

½ lb (225 g) bean sprouts

Toasted white sesame seeds, for garnish (optional)

Prepare the dressing by whisking together the ginger, vegan fish sauce, soy sauce, and sesame oil in a large bowl. Bring a pot of salted water to a vigorous simmer over high heat. Reduce the heat to medium and add the sprouts. Simmer until just tender, about 5 minutes. Drain in a colander. Add the sprouts to the dressing and stir gently until the sprouts are evenly coated. Set aside for 10 minutes at room temperature to enable the flavors to mingle before serving. Garnish with sesame seeds, if using. The sprouts will keep in a covered container in the refrigerator for a day or two but they are best when consumed fresh.

Salted Green Tea with Plant-Based Milk

SUUTEI TSAI

MONGOLIA

SERVES 4

The majority of monks in Mongolia, with its vast desert vistas and Indigenous nomadic communities, practice Vajrayana, or Tibetan Buddhism, which was introduced to the country in the 13th century CE. At Mongolian monasteries, referred to as *sum* or *khiid,* the monks, known as lamas, embrace a lifestyle of moderation, self-denial, and mental and physical austerity.

One of the most revered lamas for Mongolian Buddhists is the Tibetan guru Atiśa. His advice for living included: "The greatest achievement is selflessness. The greatest worth is self-mastery. The greatest quality is seeking to serve others. The greatest precept is continual awareness. The greatest medicine is the emptiness of everything. The greatest action is not conforming with the world's ways. The greatest magic is transmuting the passions. The greatest generosity is non-attachment."

One pleasure Mongolian Buddhist monks do not deny themselves is tea. It's especially welcome on frigid winter days. Milk has always been an important ingredient in Mongolian cuisine, where it's fermented and dried into salty cheese curds and also added to robust green and black tea that is salted to coax out deeper flavors. This recipe includes plant-based milk for a vegan alternative to traditional Mongolian suutei tsai.

1½ tablespoons green, black, or white loose-leaf tea

3 cups (720 ml) water

1 cup (240 ml) plant-based milk, such as almond, oat, soy, or whatever you prefer

½ teaspoon pink Himalayan salt

Combine the tea and water in a pot and bring to a vigorous simmer over medium-high heat. Reduce the heat to medium-low and gently simmer until the water is infused, 3–5 minutes, depending upon your strength preference. Strain the leaves from the tea and return the tea to the pot over medium heat. Add the milk and salt and return to a simmer. Remove from the heat, pour into 4 cups, and serve.

The Importance of the Tea Ceremony in Monastic Temple Cuisine

At the spiritual heart of temple cuisine, the tea ceremony plays an integral role within the ritualistic tapestry of monastic life. A manifestation of the Buddhist principles of moderation and asceticism, the tea ceremony is a meditative practice, encouraging mindfulness, gratefulness, and present-moment awareness.

Each tea ceremony includes a range of ritualistic tools—from the bamboo whisk to the tea bowl—each holding deep symbolic significance for the monks who slowly and deliberately prepare their tea each day. The ceremony itself is a beloved routine of precision, a celebration of simplicity and tranquility, mirroring the quiet rhythm of monastic life itself.

Across Asia, from the Zen temples of Japan to the high-altitude monasteries of Tibet to the expansive plateaus of Mongolia, the tea ceremony takes varied forms, reflecting local customs, culinary preferences, and culture. But at the beating heart of it, these ceremonies share common threads of peace, contemplation, ritual, gratitude, and respect for the natural world.

Monks usually partake in their tea ceremony in the early morning hours, the stillness of dawn providing a serene backdrop for this introspective ritual. The act of preparing and consuming tea serves as a metaphor for the Buddhist path, reinforcing the virtues of patience, presence, and self-restraint.

Regardless of where the Buddhist tea ceremony takes place in the world, its gentle rhythm and ancient customs, which have been embraced by monks for centuries, serve as a guide to a deeper understanding and appreciation for this spiritual practice's benevolent wisdom.

FOOD AS MEDICINE

At the foundation of monastic temple cuisine lies the profound belief that food can be a potent medicine, capable of nurturing and even healing the body, mind, and spirit. In the sacred halls of Buddhist temples, the belief that food is medicine is deeply ingrained.

Buddhist monks view food as a sacred offering, mindful of its effects on the body and mind. The key principles of this approach revolve around nourishing the body with whole and natural ingredients that promote vitality and balance. The emphasis is on fresh produce, herbs, and spices that provide essential nutrients and healing properties. By incorporating these nourishing elements, temple cuisine aims to restore harmony and promote overall well-being.

Science, too, offers profound evidence of the importance of prioritizing the notion of food as medicine. Studies have shown that certain foods have therapeutic effects, contributing to better health and disease prevention. For example, turmeric contains curcumin, a compound with powerful anti-inflammatory properties. Ginger has been found to alleviate digestive issues and reduce nausea, and leafy greens are packed with antioxidants that protect the body from harmful free radicals.

The ancient wisdom of viewing food as medicine extends far beyond the walls of the monastery, offering profound benefits to the modern person. By embracing the principles of temple cuisine, we can transform our relationship with food, cultivate a deeper understanding of the impact it has on our well-being, and begin to see food as a powerful elixir for whatever ails us.

The *Bhagavad Gita,* a sacred Hindu scripture, emphasizes the importance of a balanced and sattvic (pure) diet for overall well-being. Hindu spiritual leaders like Swami Sivananda have emphasized the concept of "food as medicine," advocating the consumption of fresh, wholesome foods that nourish the body, mind, and soul. This mindful approach to food consumption can foster a healthier relationship with food, reducing mindless consumption and promoting better digestion and optimized health. By embracing the healing properties of natural and whole ingredients cultivated within the regenerative agriculture model that gives back to the earth instead of taking its nutrients without a return, we can support our physical health and enhance our overall vitality.

The concept of food as medicine also extends to the nourishment of the spirit. By approaching meals with mindfulness and gratitude, we can create a deeper connection with our food and find moments of peace and reflection in the act of eating. This mindful approach can alleviate stress, promote emotional well-being, and improve overall mental clarity. Adopting these principles into our daily lives can foster a sense of balance, harmony, and physical and mental vitality that transcends the act of eating. When we begin to look at ingredients as nature's medicine cabinet, we strengthen not only our bodies but our minds and spirit, too.

KICHARI

INDIA

Rice and Yellow Split Peas

SERVES 4

Kichari, also spelled khichdi or kitchari, is a traditional Indian dish made from a combination of slowly stewed legumes (yellow split peas are traditionally used) and basmati rice that are cooked until a porridge–like consistency is achieved. It's considered a comfort food throughout much of India and is often consumed by monks at Buddhist temples for breakfast, lunch, or dinner. It's frequently recommended in Ayurvedic dietary practices due to its easy digestibility and balancing qualities. Spices such as turmeric, cumin, and coriander might be added for flavor, and ghee (clarified butter) is traditionally used for its health benefits. Variations of the dish might also include seasonal vegetables for added nutrition, and in this recipe vegetable oil has replaced ghee.

1 cup (200 g) yellow split peas

1 cup (200 g) basmati rice

2 teaspoons ground turmeric

1 teaspoon ground cumin

1 teaspoon ground fenugreek

1 teaspoon ground coriander

5 cups (1.2 L) water

1 teaspoon vegetable oil

1 teaspoon black mustard seeds

Salt (optional)

Plant–based yogurt, for serving (optional)

Fresh cilantro leaves, for garnish

Place the split peas in a colander and rinse them under cold running water to remove any debris. Combine the split peas, rice, turmeric, cumin, fenugreek, coriander, and water in a large pot and bring to a boil over high heat. Reduce the heat to medium–low and gently simmer until the rice is cooked through and the split peas are tender, about 45 minutes. Keep an eye on the kichari as it cooks and stir regularly to prevent it from scorching. Depending on the texture you desire, you might need to add more water, ½ cup (120 ml) at a time, if it is absorbed too quickly. When there are just a few minutes left of cooking time, heat the oil in a pan over medium heat. Add the mustard seeds and cook until the seeds begin to pop, about 1 minute. Stir into the kichari. Season to taste with salt, if desired.

To serve, ladle the kichari into 4 bowls. Top with a spoonful of plant–based yogurt, if using, and garnish with cilantro. The kichari will keep in a covered container in the refrigerator for up to 2 days.

Mahabodhi Temple

India

Located in the East Indian state of Bihar, the iconic Mahabodhi Temple in Bodh Gaya, the cradle of Buddhism, embodies a rich tapestry of historical and culinary heritage. It is here at this pilgrimage site that Siddhartha Gautama attained enlightenment beneath the sacred Bodhi tree, transforming into the Buddha more than 2,600 years ago.

The monastic cuisine at Mahabodhi echoes the Buddhist values of benevolence, gratitude, and mindfulness. It intertwines vegetarian traditions with Ayurvedic principles, viewing food as nourishment for both body and spirit. Meals might include comforting kichari (a nourishing blend of rice and lentils, page 45), flavorful subzis (vegetable curries), and the wholesome flatbread roti that the monastery's cooks imbue with medicinal herbs and spices.

The vast temple complex, a UNESCO World Heritage site that dates back to the 5th or 6th century CE, is an architectural marvel of intricately carved stone and grand stupas. A serene and welcoming atmosphere pervades the temple grounds, home to the descendants of the original Bodhi tree.

Monks and visitors alike partake in the temple's food offerings, a shared experience that fosters a sense of community. Guided by Ayurvedic wisdom, the monks at Mahabodhi Temple uphold a mindful eating practice that deeply respects life's interconnectedness, echoing the Buddha's teachings of compassion and balance. This, combined with the sacred history of the site, offers a profound spiritual and gastronomic journey for the thousands of visitors who make a pilgrimage to the temple each year.

Kimchi Soup

SERVES 6

A cornerstone of Korean monastic cuisine, jjigae, a soothing and restorative soup, is revered by Buddhist monks at Korean temples for its nutritious ingredients and warming nature, especially on cold winter evenings when the monastic halls are frigid and often wind–swept. While temple cuisine typically eschews intensely flavored aromatics like onions, garlic, and ginger (see page 29), kimchi, a staple in Korean cuisine known for its probiotic benefits and penetrating flavor, is frequently enjoyed by Korean monks who appreciate its pungency and health benefits. The tofu adds an essential boost of plant-based protein, aligning with the vegetarian lifestyle of the monks. Gochugaru is an essential and revered chile in Korea that is used for making kimchi. It can be found at most Asian specialty markets, but feel free to substitute another red chile powder or omit it, depending on your heat preference. Revered as a food with healing properties, this warming soup offers a harmonious blend of nutrition, enhancing overall well-being.

2 cups (480 ml) low-sodium vegetable broth

2 cups (480 ml) water

1 cup (200 g) vegan kimchi, chopped into bite-size pieces

¼ pound (¼ block/115 g) firm tofu, cut into ¼-inch (6-mm) squares or crumbled

1 teaspoon gochugaru

2 tablespoons fresh flat-leaf parsley leaves

Salt (optional)

1 tablespoon toasted sesame oil

In a large pot, combine the vegetable broth and water and bring to a simmer over medium heat. Add the kimchi, reduce the heat to medium-low, and continue to simmer for 10 minutes longer. Add the tofu, gochugaru, and parsley, reduce the heat to low, and simmer for 15 minutes longer. Season to taste with salt, if desired. Stir in the sesame oil, ladle the soup into warm bowls, and serve. The soup will keep in a covered container in the refrigerator for up to 3 days.

Mixed Rice Noodle Salad with Peanut Sauce

SERVES 4

Gado gado, which translates as "mix mix" in Indonesian, is a popular street food snack that is also revered by the nation's Buddhist monks for its crunchy peanuts, bright sweet-and-sour sauce, and well-rounded nutritional benefits, including healthy fats, high fiber, and vegetables that change depending on the season. Other vegetable ideas include steamed potatoes, fresh corn kernels, long beans, bean sprouts, spinach, cucumber, and cabbage. This dressing calls for brown sugar, but this could be substituted with agave or maple syrup, or omitted altogether.

FOR THE TOFU

1 block (6 oz/170 g) extra-firm tofu

1 tablespoon toasted sesame, peanut, or vegetable oil

FOR THE SAUCE

⅔ cup (185 g) peanut butter

1 tablespoon dark brown sugar, agave, or maple syrup

1 tablespoon low-sodium soy sauce

1 tablespoon tamarind pulp

1 tablespoon freshly squeezed lime juice

2 teaspoons vegan fish sauce

2 tablespoons ice water

FOR THE SALAD

1 cup (90 g) Asian pea pods

1 package (8 oz/225 g) rice noodles

Roasted peanuts, for garnish

Lime wedges, for serving

To prepare the tofu, press the tofu in a clean, dry kitchen towel to remove excess liquid, then cut it into ½-inch (12-mm) squares. Heat the oil in a pan over medium heat. Add the tofu and fry until golden brown and slightly crispy, about 4 minutes. Using a slotted spoon, transfer to a paper towel–lined plate to drain.

To prepare the sauce, in a small bowl, whisk together the peanut butter, dark brown sugar, soy sauce, tamarind, lime juice, fish sauce, and ice water until the sauce is smooth. Alternatively, blend in a food processor until smooth. Adjust the seasoning with additional sugar or lime juice, if desired.

To prepare the salad, prepare an ice bath and bring a pot of water to a simmer over medium heat. Add the pea pods to the simmering water and blanch for 1 minute. Using a spider or slotted spoon, transfer to the ice bath to stop the cooking process. Add the noodles to the simmering water and cook until tender, about 3 minutes. Drain in a colander before rinsing with cold running water to stop the cooking process and prevent the noodles from sticking together.

To serve, in a large bowl, gently toss together the fried tofu, noodles, pea pods, and half the peanut sauce until incorporated. Transfer to 4 bowls, drizzle with the remaining peanut sauce, and garnish with the roasted peanuts. Serve with lime wedges. The salad will keep in a covered container in the refrigerator for up to 1 day.

Buddha's Delight

LUÓHÀN CÀI

CHINA

SERVES 4

In the tranquil halls of Chinese temples, monks dine on humble yet vibrant meals that are in step with the seasons. Buddha's delight, or Luóhàn cài, is one such dish revered not just for its delightful taste and vibrant colors but also for its medicinal qualities. Packed with an array of seasonal vegetables like green beans, broccoli, asparagus, and carrots, it represents the harmony of nutrition and nature that monks revere. While often associated with the Lunar New Year, Buddha's delight is a versatile dish that adapts well to the seasons, shifting to include whatever fresh vegetables are available. It is a prime example of eating as an act of connection with nature and its edible medicine cabinet, a concept cherished in Buddhist kitchens throughout Asia. This colorful recipe incorporates a unique touch—rice colored with beet juice, adding an extra layer of health benefits and visual appeal. Feel free to omit this step and also try experimenting with other vegetables that celebrate the season.

---

1 cup (200 g) jasmine rice

1 cup (240 ml) water (or 2 cups/ 480 ml if not using beet juice)

1 cup (240 ml) beet juice, (preferably freshly squeezed; optional)

1 tablespoon vegetable oil

1 tablespoon minced, peeled fresh ginger

1 large carrot, thinly sliced

1 tablespoon rice vinegar

1 cup (100 g) green beans, ends trimmed if they are brown

1 cup (60 g) broccoli florets

1 cup (100 g) halved asparagus stalks

1 tablespoon low-sodium tamari or soy sauce

Place the rice in a colander and rinse it under cold running water to remove any debris. In a saucepan, combine the rice, water, and beet juice, if using, and bring to a boil over high heat. Reduce the heat to medium, cover, and simmer until the rice is tender and has absorbed all of the liquid, 15–20 minutes. Remove it from the heat and let it rest for at least 5 minutes.

In a wok or a pan, heat the oil over medium-high heat. Add the ginger and stir-fry until tender and aromatic, about 3 minutes. Add the carrot and rice vinegar and stir-fry for 2 minutes, then add the green beans, broccoli, and asparagus. Sauté the vegetables until they are just tender but still brightly colored, about 3 minutes. Add the tamari and stir-fry for 1 minute longer.

To serve, fluff the rice with a fork and spoon it into warm bowls. Spoon the vegetables alongside it and serve while still hot. Buddha's delight will keep in a covered container in the refrigerator for up to 2 days (although the vegetables will begin to lose their vibrant color and become limp over time).

Ayurvedic Cuisine

Ayurvedic cuisine, which is deeply woven into Indian culture, holds profound significance for both Buddhist monks and the nation's broader population. Rooted in history and wisdom, Ayurveda exemplifies one of the world's oldest holistic healing systems, stretching back over 5,000 years. This time-tested tradition revolves around balancing the three doshas—Vata, Pitta, and Kapha—essential energies governing our physical and mental constitution.

Incorporating Ayurvedic principles into temple cuisine transforms it into a holistic experience, harmonizing the body, mind, and spirit. Understanding each individual's unique dosha constitution enables temple cooks to craft meals promoting balance and well-being. Those with a dominant Vata dosha may benefit from grounding, warm dishes, while individuals with a prominent Pitta dosha may find cooling, soothing foods more pleasing. Aligning food choices with the prevailing dosha restores equilibrium and supports overall health.

Beyond temple walls, Ayurveda's enduring influence is hardwired into India's approach to cooking and food consumption. Contemporary households embrace Ayurvedic principles in meal planning, selecting ingredients and cooking methods aligned with their dosha constitution and the changing seasons. This timeless wisdom offers a nourishing approach that fosters balance and vitality, uniting generations.

As a holistic system, Ayurveda emphasizes the interconnectedness of mind, body, and spirit. This guiding philosophy extends to temple cuisine, where the focus shifts beyond taste to the inherent qualities and energies of ingredients. Recognizing food's potential as a source of healing and nourishment, temple cooks infuse their creations with intention and mindfulness, nurturing both the physical and the spiritual aspects of those partaking in the meals.

Ayurvedic cuisine empowers individuals to understand their body's needs and cultivate a gentle and harmonious relationship with the natural world. Emphasizing mindfulness and intention in food choices fosters well-being and balance on every level. Through the timeless wisdom of Ayurveda, temple cuisine becomes a profound journey toward holistic nourishment—a celebration of the intrinsic connection between food and the body's innate wisdom.

Pickled Plum Rice Parcels

SERVES 4

Ume onigiri, or Japanese pickled plum rice balls (or parcels in this recipe), are a beloved staple in Japanese cuisine. The tart and salty ume (pickled plum) flavor woven throughout the rice provides a satisfying taste sensation that is both comforting and invigorating. The sourness of the plums is a lovely complement for the slightly sweet flavor note of the rice and the hint of salty brine from the nori. In this recipe, umeboshi paste is combined with the rice to evenly distribute its flavor and impart a uniform festive pink color, but you can also tuck finely chopped umeboshi into the rice parcels instead (it does make for a fun discovery!).

Ume onigiri are often served at picnics in Japan and also tucked into bento boxes (see page 56). Enjoyed by Japanese monks as a quick and nourishing meal between prayers, they symbolize the simplicity and mindfulness of monastic life.

2 cups (400 g) sushi rice

2 cups (480 ml) water

3 tablespoons umeboshi paste

¼ cup (60 ml) low-sodium soy sauce

Eight 2 × 4-inch (5 × 10-cm) strips nori

Place the rice in a colander and rinse it under cold running water until the water runs clear to remove residual starch. Combine the rice and water in a saucepan and bring to a simmer over medium-high heat. Cover, reduce the heat to low, and cook until the rice is tender and has absorbed all of the liquid, 15–20 minutes. Keep covered and set aside for at least 5 minutes.

While the rice is still warm, gently stir it together with the umeboshi paste until it is evenly distributed and the rice is a uniform color. Pour the soy sauce into a small bowl. With clean, damp hands, shape the rice into 8 triangles or balls, depending on your preference. Brush all sides of one of the parcels with the soy sauce using a pastry brush and while it is still damp, shape the nori strip around it. Repeat with the remaining parcels. Allow the onigiri to cool completely before serving. They can be stored in a covered container in the refrigerator for up to 3 days.

The Bento Box
A Symbol of Japanese Culinary Tradition

A bento box is a traditional Japanese lunch box designed to hold a single-portion, balanced meal. Distinctly partitioned, it traditionally consists of rice, fish or meat, pickled or cooked vegetables, and occasionally fruits. The compartments ensure flavors remain separate, preserving the integrity of each dish. The history of the bento traces back to the Kamakura period (1192–1333 CE) in Japan. Originally, bentos were simple bags containing dried rice that could be eaten as is or rehydrated. Over time, as Japan modernized and urbanized, the bento adapted, mirroring societal changes. During the Edo period (1603–1867 CE), the culture of bento flourished, with meticulously crafted lacquerware boxes becoming popular. By the 20th century, the bento had become ubiquitous throughout Japan, reflecting both daily life and special occasions. Whether enjoyed during cherry blossom viewing or purchased at a busy train station as sustenance for a day at the office, the bento is a testament to Japan's culinary heritage and cultural legacy.

Given the Buddhist principles that often promote non-harm and reverence for all living beings, many monks adhere to a plant-based bento box. A bento box, with its partitioned spaces and balanced meal philosophy, aligns perfectly with a monk's approach to mindful eating—savoring each bite, appreciating the source of nourishment, and reflecting on the interconnectedness of life. A monk might use a bento box as a tool for meditation in action. Each compartment serves as a reminder to appreciate the sources of sustenance, the efforts that brought the food to the table, and the impermanence of life. With every bite, the monk is grounded in the present moment, cultivating gratitude and awareness. In this way, even a simple meal becomes a profound spiritual practice.

Here are twelve ideas for a monk's plant-based bento box:

Brown Rice Onigiri
Rice balls filled with umeboshi (pickled plum) for a tangy surprise (see page 55).

Tofu Steak
Pan-fried tofu marinated in tamari and ginger, offering a hearty protein source.

Vegetable Dumplings
Dumplings filled with a medley of chopped vegetables (see page 100).

Kabocha Simmer
Sweet Japanese pumpkin stewed in a light soy-mirin broth.

Nasu Dengaku
Broiled eggplant topped with a sweet miso glaze.

Seaweed Salad
Refreshing wakame seaweed with a sesame-soy dressing.

Shiitake Nimono
Mushrooms simmered in a flavorful broth until tender.

Asparagus Tempura
Tender asparagus spears in a light vegan batter, fried to crispy perfection.

Kinpira Gobo
Burdock root and carrot sautéed in a sweet soy glaze, offering a crunchy bite.

Miso Soup
A warming broth with tofu cubes, green onions, and nourishing wakame seaweed.

Daikon Pickles
Fermented radish slices that cleanse the palate and improve gut health (see page 150).

Matcha Mochi
Chewy rice cakes infused with green tea, providing a sweet finish.

Turmeric-Tamarind Juice

SERVES 2

Kunyit asam, a vibrant and tangy turmeric–tamarind beverage from Indonesia, is a popular drink at the country's Buddhist temples where turmeric and tamarind are sometimes used in Buddhist rituals and ceremonies. Both ingredients are appreciated for their nutritional benefits and healing properties that align with the Buddhist adherence to practicing mindfulness and deeply focusing on the ingredients being consumed and the benefits they provide for the body, mind, and spirit. Add a pinch of salt to each glass to further enhance the flavor.

---

2 tablespoons tamarind concentrate

4 cups (960 ml) distilled water

1 teaspoon ground turmeric

2 teaspoons brown sugar

Ice, for serving

Orange slices, for garnish

Combine the tamarind concentrate and water in a saucepan over medium heat and bring to a simmer. Whisk in the turmeric and brown sugar and continue to simmer until the sugar is dissolved, about 2 minutes. Remove from the heat and let cool. Fill 2 tall glasses with ice and pour the kunyit asam over it. Garnish with orange slices and serve. The juice will keep in a sealed pitcher in the refrigerator for up to 2 days.

The Middle Way

The Middle Way, a key concept in Buddhism, advises avoiding extreme self-indulgence and self-denial, encouraging a balanced approach to life. Originating from Buddha's first sermon post-enlightenment, it counters the extremes of hedonistic pleasure-seeking and severe asceticism prevalent during his time. Buddha's personal experiences taught him that neither extreme led to true liberation from suffering. The Middle Way promotes moderation and is encapsulated in the Noble Eightfold Path—right understanding, intention, speech, action, livelihood, effort, mindfulness, and concentration. Practicing these aids in achieving nirvana, a state free from suffering, and rebirth.

SEASONALITY

In the serene temples scattered across Asia, the monks align themselves with nature's rhythms, allowing the changing seasons to guide their food preparation and consumption, and finding harmony in the embrace of seasonal abundance.

Science offers profound evidence of the importance of eating in step with the seasons. Research demonstrates that consuming fruits and vegetables in their appropriate seasons maximizes their nutrient content. When fruits and vegetables are picked ripe and consumed soon after, they retain their peak nutritional value. In contrast, foods that are out of season or travel long distances to reach us may lose valuable nutrients during transportation and storage.

Seasonal eating also supports sustainable agricultural practices and minimizes the environmental impact of food production, principles that are prioritized by Buddhist monks. By choosing locally sourced, seasonal produce, we contribute to the preservation of biodiversity, reduce greenhouse gas emissions associated with long-distance transportation, and support local farmers and communities.

Buddhist monks have long understood the value of harmonizing with nature's cycles, and their agricultural practices reflect a deep respect for the seasons. They adhere to key principles of farming and eating in sync with nature's rhythms, embracing the ebb and flow of each season's offerings. During spring and summer, monastic gardens bloom with an array of fresh greens that nourish the body with their vibrant colors and flavors. As autumn arrives, heartier fruit varieties and root vegetables become abundant, providing sustenance to prepare for the coming winter.

Incorporating the lessons of eating with the seasons into our modern lives can lead to a deeper connection with nature, ourselves, and the people who grow our food. By choosing local, seasonal produce, we can tap into the richness of flavors and nutrients that each season offers. Our taste buds are enlivened by the sweetness of summer berries, the crispness of autumn apples, and the earthiness of winter root vegetables. Through this connection with the natural world, we can experience a profound sense of appreciation and gratitude for the gifts of the earth.

Beyond the joy of vibrant flavors, embracing seasonality can also foster a healthier and more balanced diet. As the temperatures change throughout the year, our bodies naturally crave different foods. In summer, lighter and refreshing dishes help us stay cool, while heartier meals in winter provide warmth and comfort. By listening to our bodies' cues and aligning our food choices with the seasons, we can support our overall well-being and optimize our nutritional intake.

By savoring the bounty that each season offers, we honor the cycle of life, nurture our bodies, and celebrate the vibrant flavors that nature provides. We discover and benefit from the abundance and harmony in aligning our plates with the ever-changing dance of the seasons.

Noodles with Vegetables

SERVES 4

Pad thai jay is a vegan variant of traditional pad thai, adhering to the Buddhist dietary practice, *jay,* that embodies the principle of avoiding animal products and strong-smelling vegetables. Tofu replaces meat, with alternatives like soy sauce and vegan fish sauce for flavor. Key pad thai elements like stir-fried rice noodles and tamarind remain. Monks in Thailand relish this recipe for its nutritional benefits, the vibrant blend of ingredients that change with the seasons, and the refreshing burst of flavor it delivers.

---

1 package (7 oz/200 g) pad thai noodles

1 tablespoon peanut or vegetable oil

1 package (8 oz/225 g) extra-firm tofu, cut into bite-size pieces

1 carrot, shredded

1 rib celery, thinly sliced

2 cups (70 g) seasonal greens such as spinach or bok choy, coarsely chopped

½ cup (85 g) finely chopped peanuts

1 tablespoon low-sodium soy sauce

1 tablespoon vegan fish sauce

1 tablespoon freshly squeezed lime juice

1 tablespoon tamarind pulp

⅔ cup (26 g) bean sprouts

Thinly sliced red chiles, for garnish (optional)

Lime wedges, for serving

Soak the noodles in hot water until they are tender, about 15 minutes. Drain. While the noodles are soaking, heat the oil in a wok or pan over medium heat. Add the tofu and stir-fry until golden brown and slightly crispy, about 5 minutes. Transfer to a paper towel–lined plate using a slotted spoon to drain.

Add the carrot and celery to the pan and stir-fry until the carrot is just tender, about 5 minutes. Add the greens and peanuts and stir-fry for 2 minutes longer. Add the noodles, tofu, soy sauce, vegan fish sauce, lime juice, and tamarind and sauté for 3 minutes longer.

Remove from the heat and stir in the bean sprouts. Spoon into warm bowls, garnish with chiles, if using, and serve with lime wedges. The noodles will keep in a covered container in the refrigerator for up to 2 days.

Wat Phra That Doi Suthep
Thailand

Situated high in the lush green mountains of northern Thailand, Wat Phra That Doi Suthep, near the bustling city of Chiang Mai, is a stunning testament to the region's long and rich Buddhist heritage. Established in the 14th century CE, the temple stands as an exquisite example of Thai architecture, with its glistening golden *chedi* (stupa) and intricate *naga* (serpent) statues.

The culinary traditions of the temple mirror the region's focus on seasonality, drawing upon a bounty of locally sourced produce, including mangoes, lychees, papayas, Thai basil, bok choy, and lemongrass. The monks prepare dishes like gaeng som (sour curry) and pad pak ruam (stir-fried mixed vegetables) using ingredients harvested at their peak of the season for maximum flavor and nutritional value.

The monks' adherence to the concept of seasonal cooking aligns with Buddhist teachings on mindfulness and respect for nature's rhythms. This connection between food and spirituality is further showcased when the monks share their vegetarian meals with visitors, fostering a sense of community and cultural exchange.

The agricultural traditions near the temple reflect a harmonious blend of traditional farming and sustainable practices, emphasizing crops that thrive in each season. The cuisine at Doi Suthep is not only a flavorful feast for the palate and a colorful mosaic for the eyes, but also a reflection of the surrounding landscape and its cyclical patterns, enhancing the temple's tranquil ambience and providing a unique culinary experience rooted in Buddhist principles.

Mashed Sweet Potatoes

KEWA KATSA
BHUTAN

SERVES 4

Buddhism is the national religion of the mountainous nation called Bhutan. Most Bhutanese people practice Vajrayana Buddhism, which is also referred to as Tibetan Buddhism. Even Bhutan's traditional name, Druk Yul, which translates as "Land of the Thunder Dragon," has its roots in Buddhism, where the dragon symbolizes wisdom, transformation, elemental forces, and subduing negative emotions, which are all important Buddhist principles. Bhutan's prioritization of the Buddhist philosophy of sustainability, spiritual fulfillment over material wealth, and holistic well-being is reflected in its national development philosophy of Gross National Happiness (GNP). For the monks of Bhutan's Buddhist temples scattered throughout its soaring mountaintops, seasonality and eating in step with nature and the harvest are key to their cooking practices. Sweet potatoes are harvested in late fall and early winter and are appreciated for the sustenance they provide during Bhutan's bitter-cold winter season. Kewa katsa typically includes white potatoes, but sweet potatoes add a vibrant pop of color and a sweeter flavor.

4 sweet potatoes
(about 5 oz/140 g each)

Vegetable oil, as needed

Salt and freshly ground black pepper

½ teaspoon ground turmeric

½ teaspoon ground coriander

¼ teaspoon red chile powder (optional)

Fresh cilantro leaves, for garnish (optional)

Preheat the oven to 400°F (200°C). Scrub the potatoes under cold running water to remove residue and pat them dry using a kitchen towel. Rub the potatoes with oil and season with salt and pepper. Wrap each individually in aluminum foil, place on a baking sheet, and roast until they are fork-tender, 40–50 minutes, depending on their size. Remove from the oven and let cool. Once they are cool enough to handle, remove the peels and compost them (or save for later use). In a large bowl, combine the potatoes, turmeric, coriander, and chile powder, if using, and mash using a fork until incorporated but still a bit chunky. Season to taste with salt and pepper and garnish with cilantro, if desired. Leftovers will keep in a covered container in the refrigerator for up to 3 days.

Lotus Seed Congee

SERVES 4

Congee is a comforting and adaptable rice porridge that holds a cherished place in the culinary traditions of monks throughout Asia, including those in Chinese Buddhist temples. This dish's simplicity embodies the Buddhist principles of modesty, nourishment, and frugality, while its adaptability makes it an ideal vessel for seasonal ingredients. Aside from this lotus seed version, you might consider variations with adzuki beans for a sweet twist, shiitake mushrooms for a savory umami kick, or even mung beans for an added layer of texture. Lotus seeds are deeply symbolic in Buddhism, representing spiritual growth and purity of the spirit, mirroring the plant's journey from its muddy depths of origin to a resplendent flower, reminding us that we have the ability to rise and bloom no matter what our starting point.

---

1 cup (100 g) dehydrated lotus seeds

1 cup (200 g) jasmine rice

8 cups (1.9 L) water

Salt

Crunchy sea salt, for serving

Toasted chopped walnuts, for serving (optional)

Goji berries, for serving (optional)

Honey, agave, or maple syrup, for serving

Soak the lotus seeds in water until they are soft and puffy, about 4 hours. Drain. Place the rice in a colander and rinse under cold running water until the water runs clear to remove excess starch. In a pot, combine the rice, rehydrated lotus seeds, and 4 cups (960 ml) of the water and bring to a vigorous simmer over high heat.

Reduce the heat to low, partially cover, and gently simmer until the rice has absorbed most of the liquid, stirring occasionally to prevent scorching. Add the remaining water, ½ cup (120 ml) at a time, simmering and stirring until the liquid is almost absorbed before adding the next portion. The texture of your congee will vary depending upon the texture you prefer. Either cook it until the rice is completely broken down and the texture is runny like loose oatmeal or add less water and cook it a bit less for a more solid, thick, and creamy version.

Once it has reached your desired consistency, remove the congee from the heat and season to taste with salt. Spoon into warm bowls. Sprinkle with crunchy sea salt and, if desired, garnish with walnuts and goji berries and drizzle with honey.

Seasonal Buddhist Celebrations and Traditions

Buddhism is steeped in the rhythms and transformation of nature throughout the year. Disciples mark the dependable staccato of the changing seasons with countless ceremonies and traditions, marking important teachings of the Buddha and celebrating the unique aspects of each season.

In Sri Lanka and many parts of Asia, the Vesak festival during the first full moon in May celebrates Buddha's birth, enlightenment, and death. Devotees, even if they are not strict vegetarians, often abstain from meat and dairy products during this time, enjoying vegan meals while quenching their thirst with sweet beverages that feel celebratory, like botanical teas and panakam, a jaggery-based drink.

The Rain Retreat, or "Vassa," lasts for three lunar months during the rainy season (usually July to October) in many parts of Asia. Monks often remain inside their monasteries during this reflective time, focusing on meditation and teaching. The community supports them by offering food and naturally dyed robes. At the conclusion of the retreat, the Kathina ceremony is the time when the monks receive their new robes and share a communal meal with the devotees who cared for them.

The Buddhist Moon Festival, or Mid-Autumn Festival, is celebrated in East Asia on the 15th day of the 8th lunar month. Originating in China as a harvest festival, it includes offerings to Buddha and the Moon Goddess. The festival is notably marked by consuming lotus paste or salted egg yolk-stuffed mooncakes, their round shape symbolizing completeness and reunion.

These celebrations that delineate the changing seasons are not only spiritual milestones but also affirm the interconnectedness and flow of life and nature. Seasonal foods and customs reflect Buddhist principles of mindfulness, community, and gratitude, reminding devotees of the transient, cyclical nature of life, central to Buddhist philosophy. They enable each season's passing to become a mindful reflection and celebration of life's impermanent beauty.

Cherry Blossom Soda

SERVES 2

Cherry blossoms, or sakura, hold deep cultural and spiritual significance in Japan. Revered by Zen Buddhists for their ephemeral beauty, they bloom briefly in the spring, flooding the landscape in a wash of optimistic pink, usually between late March and early April, symbolizing the fleeting nature of life itself. Monks have traditionally observed sakura trees for meditative contemplation, embodying "mono no aware," the awareness of impermanence. This awareness of the transience of beauty and life heightens its preciousness, stirring emotions that range from happiness to a wistful sadness, something deeply embedded in Zen teachings. Harvesting these delicate blossoms at their peak is a mindful practice, and monks treat this activity with respect and reverence for nature and its endless gifts. This recipe calls for sakura extract, which is readily available at Asian specialty markets. Of course, if you are fortunate enough to catch the cherry blossoms in bloom, feel free to forage for them and make this extract yourself.

Ice, for serving

1 tablespoon sakura extract

1 tablespoon simple syrup (optional)

Sparkling water, for serving

Organic pink flowers, for garnish (optional)

Fill 2 highball glasses with ice and add half of the sakura extract and simple syrup, if using, to each glass. Top with enough sparkling water to fill the glasses and gently stir until the liquid turns a blush pink color. Garnish with a sakura blossom or another pink flower and serve.

Green Papaya Salad

SERVES 4

Som tum jay is a refreshing and tangy green papaya salad that is a staple at temples throughout Thailand, where it is enjoyed by monks and monastic visitors alike. Thailand's tropical climate is conducive to papaya growth all year long, which makes this zesty and refreshing salad a welcome accompaniment to seasonal delicacies any time of year. This recipe calls for garlic and Thai red chiles, but if you prefer to adhere to the monastic avoidance of overpowering flavors, feel free to omit them.

1 large green papaya, peeled, cored, and shredded

2 carrots, shredded

1 cup (170 g) quartered cherry tomatoes

1 tablespoon minced garlic

2 Thai red chiles, thinly sliced

1 tablespoon sugar

1 tablespoon tamarind concentrate

1 tablespoon low-sodium soy sauce

1 tablespoon freshly squeezed lime juice

2 teaspoons vegan fish sauce

Salt

2/3 cup (80 g) coarsely chopped cashews

In a large bowl, gently toss together the papaya, carrots, and tomatoes. Using a mortar and pestle, crush together the garlic and chiles until they form a coarse paste. Transfer to a large bowl and whisk it together with the sugar, tamarind concentrate, soy sauce, lime juice, and vegan fish sauce until the sugar is dissolved. Add the shredded vegetables and gently toss until well coated. Season to taste with salt. Set aside at room temperature for at least 15 minutes to encourage the flavors to mingle. Spoon into 4 bowls and sprinkle each salad with the cashews before serving. The salad will keep in a covered container in the refrigerator for up to 1 day but is best enjoyed immediately when the papaya is crisp and fresh.

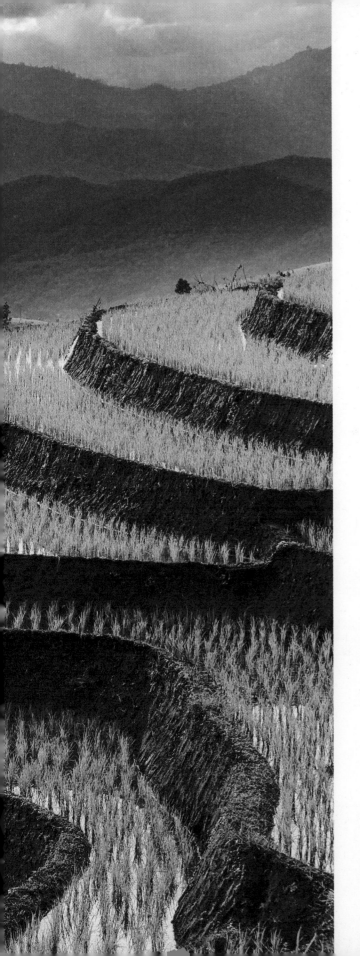

How to Bring Nature and Seasonal Beauty to a Monastic-Inspired Table

Bringing monastic inspirations and Buddhist principles to your dining table means embracing simplicity, mindfulness, and the beauty of nature and the changing seasons. Start with a clean, uncluttered table, reflecting the monastic principle of simplicity. Use a naturally colored tablecloth or place mats made from materials such as bamboo or linen to evoke a connection to nature.

Introduce elements that celebrate the season. In springtime, flower or vegetable blossoms or fresh green leaves can be an unfussy but jubilant centerpiece; in summertime, add a bowl of seasonal fruit at their peak freshness, which will not only add color but also tantalizing aroma; autumn could feature seasonal apples, pumpkins, or gourds or vibrant fallen leaves; and winter could include foraged evergreen sprigs or pine cones.

Use dishes and utensils that feel good in the hand, perhaps handmade pottery glazed with warm, neutral shades that would be found in the natural world or hand-carved wooden utensils. This encourages mindfulness and appreciation of the artisan who created it, a nod to the monastic tradition of self-sufficiency and craftsmanship. As you're setting your table, remember that the goal is to create a peaceful, uncluttered, and inviting space that encourages mindful eating and reflects the transient beauty of nature and the changing seasons.

Rice and Nori Rolls

SERVES 4

Eating in step with the seasons is a priority for Korean monks, who have an abiding respect for nature and its cycles, as showcased in their kimbap—a dish underscoring simplicity, adaptability, and seasonal eating. *Kim* signifies seaweed and *bap* represents rice, with the ingredients selected reflecting the seasonal rhythms of nature. Each kimbap roll is more than food—it's a spiritual link to nature's heartbeat.

Often likened to sushi, kimbap carves out its own identity. Its fillings, which can be tofu or kimchi or other pickled vegetables for vegetarians, change with the seasons. This recipe calls for a bamboo mat to assist with rolling. If you don't have one, you can substitute a stiff yet pliable place mat lined with plastic wrap. This recipe includes danmuji, which is a sweet and tangy yellow pickled radish available at Asian specialty markets. If you are unable to source it, substitute another pickled vegetable like daikon or cucumber. Other seasonal vegetable ideas include spinach, bok choy, avocado, and bell peppers.

4 cups (620 g) cooked sushi rice (see page 55)

3 tablespoons white sesame seeds

1½ tablespoons sesame oil

1 teaspoon kosher salt

4 sheets nori

¼ lb (115 g) danmuji, julienned

1 carrot, julienned

1 cucumber, julienned

Gently stir together the rice, 2 tablespoons of the sesame seeds, sesame oil, and salt in a bowl. Lay a sheet of nori at the edge of a bamboo sushi mat. Spread about a ½-inch (12-mm) layer of rice evenly over the nori, leaving about 1 inch (2.5 cm) of space at the top of the sheet to seal the roll. Arrange one-fourth of the danmuji, carrot, and cucumber horizontally across the center of the rice layer. Using the bamboo mat, roll your kimbap using even pressure throughout the process to ensure that the roll is tight and holds together. Once it is rolled, wet the exposed portion at the edge of the nori and then seal the roll.

Carefully unroll the mat and set the kimbap aside on a cutting board while you repeat the process for the remaining kimbap. Once this step is completed, use a sharp knife to slice each roll into thirds. Transfer to a serving platter, sprinkle with the remaining 1 tablespoon of sesame seeds, and serve. Kimbap will keep in a covered container in the refrigerator for up to 2 days.

RITUAL & ROUTINE

At the heart of temple cuisine lies the practice of ritual and routine—a deep-seated belief system especially ingrained in Zen Buddhism. Japanese Buddhist monk Shunryu Suzuki once eloquently expressed, "In the beginner's mind there are many possibilities, but in the expert's there are few." This sentiment exemplifies the significance of approaching food with a sense of established rituals and positive routines that eventually become innate superpowers in our eating habits.

Zen Buddhist monks find solace in the sacredness of routine, which extends to the tasks of growing food. Each step, from planting the seeds to nurturing the crops, is imbued with intention and mindfulness. The process becomes a meditative practice, fostering a deep connection with the earth and the cycles of nature. Through this ritualistic approach to food cultivation, Zen Buddhist monks find a profound sense of purpose and harmony with the natural world, empowering themselves with the virtue of routine.

Similarly, in the art of food preparation and consumption, ritual and routine play a central role. Monks embrace simplicity in their culinary practices, focusing on basic ingredients to create nourishing meals. Being fully present during food preparation without allowing the mind to wander becomes a meditative act, where each slice, chop, and stir is performed with care and intention. In the serene setting of the monastic dining hall, the act of eating itself becomes a ritual, a moment of gratitude and presence. Monks savor each bite mindfully, fully immersing themselves in the experience and fostering a deeper connection with the nourishment they receive.

Incorporating food rituals and routines into our daily lives can have profound benefits for our health and mental well-being. By adopting a more mindful approach to food cultivation and preparation, we nurture a deeper connection with the earth and the nourishment it provides. Ritualistic eating practices allow us to slow down, savor the flavors, and appreciate the nourishment we receive. It also strengthens our spirits by giving us something to depend on, which makes us feel comforted and secure. Ritual and routine can reduce stress, improve digestion, and foster a greater sense of contentment in our daily lives.

The wisdom of incorporating ritual and routine into food growing, preparation, and consumption extends far beyond the walls of the monastery. In our modern lives, we can infuse mindfulness into every meal, creating moments of nourishment and gratitude where we are fully present and in tune with the beauty of the recipe in front of us. Eating in this way offers a more meaningful and fulfilling approach to food, rooted in the timeless wisdom of ritual and routine.

Hibiscus Tea

SERVES 4

The hibiscus flower, referred to as *rumduol* in the Khmer language, is the national flower of Cambodia. This delicate, ruby red beauty is an integral part of many Cambodian cultural and Buddhist religious ceremonies and rituals, where it is revered not only for its radiance but also for its association with purity, love, and good fortune. This symbol of cultural pride is also an integral part of Khmer traditional medicine, where it is used in teas and herbal remedies designed to soothe, cool, and cleanse the body. Bon chruk chet is routinely served at meals enjoyed at Buddhist temples throughout Cambodia and also offered as a welcoming drink to visitors. Dried hibiscus flowers can be found at most Asian specialty markets.

---

4 cups (960 ml) distilled water

⅔ cup (25 g) dried hibiscus flowers, plus 4 more to garnish

In a pot, bring the water to a boil over high heat. Reduce the heat to medium and add the hibiscus. Simmer for 5 minutes while stirring with a wooden spoon to encourage the hibiscus flowers to release their color and flavor. Remove from the heat and let cool. Strain into a pitcher and refrigerate until chilled. Garnish with one of the dried hibiscus flowers for a celebratory finish. The tea will keep in a sealed pitcher in the refrigerator for up to 2 weeks.

Tenryu-ji Temple
Japan

Founded in 1339 CE, Tenryu-ji Temple, a UNESCO World Heritage site nestled in Kyoto's scenic Arashiyama district, is a cornerstone of Zen Buddhism and its culinary tradition of Shōjin Ryōri. This vegetarian cuisine reflects the Zen principles of simplicity and mindfulness, with meals prepared and consumed in a ritualized manner to rein in the wandering mind and foster spiritual growth.

During their daily routine, the temple's monks create meals that are a meditation in themselves, turning humble, seasonal ingredients into dishes such as yudofu (simmered tofu) and ohitashi (simmered seasonal greens flavored with soy sauce) with deliberate, measured actions. Seasonal vegetables, tofu, and fermented items feature heavily, respecting the natural bounty of each season.

Tenryu-ji's meticulously landscaped garden, Sōgenchi, with its central pond mirroring the surrounding mountains, offers visitors a tranquil dining experience at the temple's Shigetsu restaurant. Guests enjoy a Shōjin Ryōri meal, which enables them to experience the Zen philosophy of respect for all life forms, the cyclical nature of existence, and interconnectivity.

The temple's history and architecture, including the main hall and the hojo (abbot's quarters), are testimony to its rich and long-standing heritage. Amid the breathtaking natural beauty of Arashiyama, Tenryu-ji is a conduit for visitors to explore the intersection of Zen principles, ritualized cuisine, and mindful eating.

TOM KHA
THAILAND

Galangal Soup

SERVES 4

Tom kha soup, a sweet-and-sour staple in Thai cuisine, has a special place in the daily lives of Thai Buddhist monks. They rely heavily on the ritual of alms-gathering (see page 20) for their meals, and tom kha soup, with its balance of readily available, nutrient-dense ingredients, aligns perfectly with the simplicity and mindfulness of their lifestyle.

This recipe calls for galangal, a root similar to ginger and turmeric and in the same family, but it has a unique flavor that's hard to replicate. It's commonly used in Thai and Indonesian cooking. It's readily available at Asian specialty markets, but if you can't find fresh or dried galangal, the most common substitute is ginger. Keep in mind that ginger has a spicier, slightly sweeter flavor compared to the more citrusy and earthy flavor of galangal. For a closer match, you could combine the ginger with a bit of lemon zest. While this substitute mimics the flavor of galangal to some extent, it won't perfectly replicate its unique taste.

---

2 cans (14 oz/400 g) coconut milk

2 stalks lemongrass, tough outer layers removed and tender part thinly sliced

2 inches (5 cm) fresh ginger, peeled and minced

4 inches (10 cm) fresh galangal, peeled and minced

1½ cups (135 g) fresh shiitake mushrooms, brushed clean and thinly sliced

1 cup (90 g) bamboo shoots

2 tablespoons vegan fish sauce

3 cups (90 g) loosely packed fresh baby spinach, coarsely chopped

Juice of 1 lime

Fresh cilantro, for garnish (optional)

In a large pot over medium-high heat, combine the coconut milk, lemongrass, ginger, and galangal and bring to a vigorous simmer. Reduce the heat to medium-low and gently simmer for 10 minutes to infuse the flavors. Add the shiitake mushrooms and bamboo shoots and simmer until the vegetables are tender, about 10 minutes. Add the vegan fish sauce and spinach and simmer until the spinach begins to wilt, about 3 minutes. Remove from the heat and stir in the lime juice. Ladle the soup into warm bowls and garnish with cilantro, if desired. The soup will keep in a covered container in the refrigerator for up to 3 days.

Kaiseki and Shōjin Ryōri Cuisine

Kaiseki and Shōjin Ryōri represent the harmonious confluence of culinary art and Zen Buddhism in Japan. Both embody the principles of respect for nature, mindful food preparation, and meditative consumption that provide a path for spiritual cultivation.

Shōjin Ryōri, originating in Zen temples, is strictly vegetarian (and typically vegan), symbolizing nonviolence and reverence for all life forms. Its dishes, often centered on tofu, seaweed, preserved ingredients, and seasonal vegetables, abide by the principle of balance in taste, color, and method of preparation. This creates a cohesive medley of diverse yet harmonious flavors prepared using simple ingredients, a reflection of Buddhist philosophies of interconnectedness and harmony.

Kaiseki, despite evolving into a sophisticated dining style served in ryokans (traditional Japanese inns that originated in the Edo period from 1603–1867 CE) and high-end restaurants, has its roots in the austere tea ceremony meals of Buddhist temples. Like Shōjin Ryōri cuisine, it embraces seasonality, with each dish reflecting the transient beauty of the seasons, and follows a fixed sequence of courses, emphasizing a ritualistic presentation.

In the Zen temple, the tenzo, or the cook who is also a monk, plays a pivotal role in these culinary traditions. The tenzo's work is a spiritual practice, their mindful and focused preparation embodying the Zen priority of being present in the moment. This mindfulness translates into the food, transforming each meal into a transcendent, meditative experience that clears the mind of clutter and frees the spirit from anything that is unnecessary.

Both Kaiseki and Shōjin Ryōri offer more than sustenance. They nurture being present and cultivating the discipline of gratitude, vital to Zen practice, and instill a deeper appreciation for the natural world. They highlight the act of eating as a spiritual endeavor and reflect the essence of Zen: finding extraordinary beauty in our ordinary, everyday lives.

Steamed Bun Sandwiches

SERVES 4

Bao, or as it's sometimes called in Taiwan, baozi, is a quintessential part of Taiwanese food culture. These steamed buns are prevalent throughout the nation, sold in night markets, roadside stalls, and traditional restaurants, and enjoyed by monks at the temples.

The bao is made from scratch in this recipe; it might seem like a fussy step, but kneading the dough, giving it time to rise, and then watching it puff up when it's steamed is a rewarding ritual that is worth the effort. If you don't have time for this step, premade bao are readily available at Asian specialty markets. Of course, as with so many monastic recipes, the ingredients reflect the season, so feel free to let the availability at your local farmers' market guide your gua bao experience. A bamboo steamer is called for, but a stainless steel steamer could also be used. If you don't own a steamer, see page 130 for using a homemade steamer.

FOR THE DOUGH

4 cups (460 g) all-purpose flour, plus flour as needed

1 tablespoon sugar

1 tablespoon active dry yeast

1 cup (240 ml) warm water

To prepare the dough, in a large bowl, combine the flour, sugar, and yeast. Slowly add the warm water and gently knead the dough on a clean, lightly floured work surface until it is smooth and elastic and resembles pizza dough or bread dough. Place the dough in a lightly oiled bowl large enough to hold it and enable it to double in size. Place a damp kitchen towel over the bowl and let the dough rest until it doubles in size and is smooth and pillowy, about 2 hours.

Recipe continues

FOR THE FILLING

1 cup (60 g) finely shredded iceberg lettuce

1 large carrot, finely shredded

½ cup (15 g) loosely packed fresh cilantro leaves

1 tablespoon black sesame seeds

1 tablespoon white sesame seeds

½ cup (120 ml) hoisin sauce

2 tablespoons low-sodium soy sauce

1½ tablespoons toasted sesame oil

Juice of 1 lime

½ lb (225 g) seitan, sliced and grilled, steamed, baked, or fried

Sixteen ¼-inch (6-mm) cucumber slices

Once the dough has risen, use a bench scraper or sharp knife to divide it into 8 equal pieces. Roll each segment into a ball and then gently press it with the palm of your hand into a flat circle about 1 inch (2.5 cm) thick. Fold the circle over into a semicircle shape and transfer to a lightly oiled sheet pan or a wooden cutting board lightly dusted with flour. Cover with a damp cloth and let rise for 30 minutes. Once the buns are ready, arrange your steamer and bring water to a vigorous boil over high heat. Arrange your bao in the steamer (you might have to work in two batches depending upon the steamer size) and steam until the bao are puffy and cooked through, about 15 minutes. Carefully remove from the steamer and let rest until they have cooled.

To prepare the filling, while the bao cools, toss together the lettuce, carrot, and cilantro in a bowl and then stir in the sesame seeds, hoisin, soy sauce, sesame oil, and lime juice until incorporated. To assemble the gua bao, cut each bao open so it resembles a taco. Build your bao with a few slices of seitan, 2 cucumber slices, and a spoonful of the filling. Repeat with the remaining bao. The constructed bao should be served immediately, or if you would like to prepare the ingredients ahead of time, keep your bao and your fillings in separate covered containers in the refrigerator for up to 1 day.

More Bao Ideas

Bao are infinitely flexible and provide an excellent blank canvas for sandwich creativity. Here are a few more ideas for plant-based gua bao fillings:

Grilled Eggplant and Red Pepper
Grilled slices of eggplant and red bell peppers dressed with a light soy and sesame dressing.

Braised Tofu and Mushrooms
Slow-cooked firm tofu and mushrooms in a savory sauce, a perfect blend of sweet and salty.

Pickled Radish and Carrot
A tangy filling made with pickled daikon radish (see page 150) and carrots pickled in vinegar, sugar, and a touch of salt (see page 158).

Spicy Kimchi and Seitan
A zesty mix of fermented cabbage (vegan kimchi) and seitan, a protein-rich wheat gluten.

Sweet Potato and Black Bean
A hearty filling made from mashed sweet potatoes (see page 71) and black beans with a hint of spice.

Sautéed Bok Choy and Ginger
Lightly sautéed bok choy with fresh ginger and a splash of soy sauce for a light, refreshing filling.

Roasted Brussels Sprouts and Chile Sauce
Oven-roasted brussels sprouts drizzled with a spicy chile sauce for a flavorful kick.

Miso-Glazed Tempeh and Cabbage
Tempeh slices marinated in miso paste and then grilled until crisp, served with fresh cabbage.

Stir-Fried Green Beans and Garlic
Crisp green beans stir-fried with garlic and a dash of soy sauce for a simple yet flavorful filling.

Peanut Butter and Jelly with Banana
A fun twist on a classic—a generous smear of peanut butter, a layer of fruit jelly, and slices of fresh banana for a sweet, indulgent sandwich.

Additional Notes on Gua Bao

Sometimes referred to as a "Taiwanese hamburger," the gua bao is different from traditional closed buns, which are similar to dumplings. It's an open, taco-like bun that's typically filled with meat, pickled mustard greens, cilantro, and ground peanuts. The contrast between the soft, sweet white bun and the savory filling makes for a satisfying and fun eating experience. Taiwanese gua bao also feature unique ingredients in their fillings, such as local mushrooms, Taiwanese cabbage, or regional sauces and spices. As is common in Taiwanese cuisine, there is a harmonious blend of sweet, salty, sour, and spicy flavors present in the bao, reflecting the island's culinary diversity and creative approach to cooking.

In many Buddhist traditions, including those in China and Taiwan, where monks often adhere to a diet that is vegetarian or vegan as part of the practice of ahimsa, this belief system extends to the bao that they enjoy, which are filled with vegetarian or vegan ingredients. A typical vegetarian bao might include ingredients such as mushrooms, tofu, or various types of cooked or pickled vegetables. Some bao might even be sweet on special occasions like feast days or holidays. These delicacies are filled with bean paste, lotus seed paste, or other sweet ingredients.

Monks in Taiwan would typically eat bao as a component of their two main meals, which usually take place before midday. The act of preparing the bao, with its careful folding and steaming, could also be seen as a form of ritual that enhances the mindfulness practice. It's also worth noting that in Buddhism, food is often seen as a way to cultivate generosity and community. Bao, with its combination of simple ingredients and careful preparation, is a good example of this. It's a humble food that can be shared and enjoyed together, strengthening the bonds of the monastic community.

Vegetarian Dumplings

SERVES 4

Originating from China, jiaozi (dumplings) have become an integral part of the culinary fabric in many parts of Asia, including Singapore, where they're fondly known as su jiaozi when they are vegetarian. This recipe is not only a crowd-pleaser but also encapsulates the essence of Singapore's rich and diverse food culture. Buddhist monks in Singapore often indulge in these comforting and healthful parcels, with their commitment to non-harm mirrored in su jiaozi. The act of making and eating su jiaozi harmonizes with the Buddhist principles of ritual and routine, as the pleating of each dumpling requires mindful attention, much like meditation, promoting a sense of peace and tranquility.

Su jiaozi are also a way to build community through the act of sharing them from a communal platter. Of course, they are also a lovely way to celebrate the shifting seasons, so feel free to get creative with the filling by finding inspiration at your local markets or, if you're fortunate enough, in your own garden. This recipe calls for a bamboo steamer, but feel free to use a stainless steel steamer instead. If you don't own a steamer, see page 130 for using a homemade steamer.

For the Wrappers

2 cups (230 g) all-purpose flour, plus flour as needed

½ teaspoon salt

About ¾ cup (180 ml) warm water

To prepare the wrappers, sift together the flour and salt in a large bowl. Slowly add the warm water while incorporating it with a fork until the dough has come together and is smooth but not sticky. You might need a bit more or less water to achieve the desired consistency.

Lightly dust a clean work surface with flour. Knead the dough until it is smooth and elastic, 6–8 minutes. If the dough is too sticky after the initial kneading process, sprinkle it with flour and continue to knead. Shape the dough into a smooth ball and place it back in the bowl. Cover the top of the bowl with a damp kitchen towel and let it rest for 45 minutes. This step relaxes the gluten, making the rolling process easier.

Recipe continues

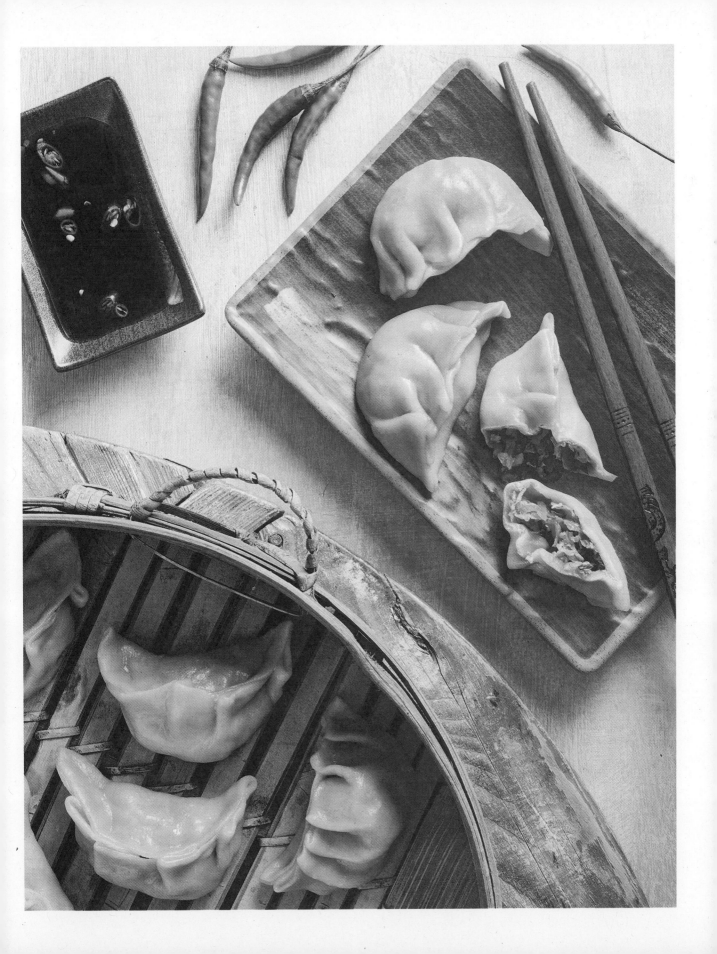

FOR THE FILLING

2 cups (180 g) finely shredded
napa cabbage

1 cup (110 g) finely shredded
carrot

½ cup (15 g) loosely packed
fresh cilantro

2 tablespoons soy sauce,
plus soy sauce as needed

2 tablespoons rice vinegar

2 tablespoons toasted
sesame oil

After the dough has rested, light dust the work surface with flour. Using a bench scraper or sharp knife, cut the dough in half. Place one section back in the bowl and cover with the damp kitchen towel to keep it from drying out. Roll the dough into a 12-inch (12.5-cm) long cylinder and then cut it into 1-inch (2.5-cm) segments. Roll one of the segments into a ball and then roll it out into a circle that is 3 to 4 inches (7.5 to 10 cm) in diameter. Repeat the process with the remaining segments and then with the remaining dough. At this stage you can either fill the dumplings right away (see below) or stack them on a plate, placing a piece of parchment paper between each wrapper to prevent them from sticking together. If you would like to make your wrappers ahead of time, they can be refrigerated at this stage in a covered container for up to 2 days or frozen for up to 30 days.

To prepare the filling, in a large bowl, combine the cabbage, carrot, and cilantro. In a separate bowl, stir together the soy sauce, rice vinegar, and sesame oil and then pour it over the vegetables and toss until everything is well coated.

Place a small bowl of warm water on a clean work station and arrange your dumpling wrappers on it. Place a small spoonful of the filling in the center of a wrapper. Dip your finger in the water and run it along the edge of the wrapper to moisten it. Fold the wrapper over to create a half-moon shape and then press the edges together to seal it. To create a pleated design, give a tiny twist to each portion of the wrapper as it's pressed. Repeat with the remaining wrappers and filling. At this stage, if you would like to finish your dumplings at a later time, they will keep in a covered container in the refrigerator for up to 3 days.

Prepare your steamer and then bring water to a boil over high heat. Arrange your dumplings in the steamer (you may have to work in two batches depending upon the steamer size) and steam until the wrappers begin to turn translucent, about 15 minutes. Serve on a platter with soy sauce (or your preferred sauce; see page 135 for a list of plant-based dipping sauces)

Braised Greens

SERVES 4

This delicately braised spinach recipe is a key component of Japanese Shōjin Ryōri cuisine (see page 92), a style of vegetarian food preparation originating in Buddhist temples. This dish reflects the Shōjin Ryōri principles of simple, natural ingredients comprising balanced meals that are nourishing and easily digestible. *Horenso,* which refers to spinach, and *nimono,* which means gently braised or simmered, is a component of Shōjin Ryōri culinary rituals that reflect the harmonious gratitude for nature that defines this enlightened form of Japanese cooking. This dish calls for spinach, but feel free to substitute other greens, such as baby kale, beet leaves, or the leafy green portion of bok choy. For a little texture, sprinkle with black or white sesame seeds.

8 cups (240 g) loosely packed fresh spinach

¼ cup (60 ml) dashi or vegetable broth

1 tablespoon low-sodium soy sauce

1 tablespoon mirin

Toasted sesame oil, as needed

Black or white sesame seeds, for garnish (optional)

Rinse the spinach under cold running water to remove debris and pat dry with a kitchen towel. Remove the stems from the spinach and either compost or save for a different use. Tear the spinach leaves into bite-size pieces. Prepare an ice bath and bring a pot of water to a boil over high heat. Add the spinach all at once to the boiling water and blanch until the spinach is a bright electric green color, about 30 seconds. Transfer to the ice water using a spider or a slotted spoon.

While the spinach cools, combine the dashi, soy sauce, and mirin in a pot and bring to a simmer over medium heat. Remove the spinach from the ice water and squeeze dry to remove as much liquid as possible. Add the spinach to the simmering liquid and cook until heated through while stirring gently with a wooden spoon, about 2 minutes.

Remove the spinach from the liquid using a slotted spoon and distribute among 4 bowls. Drizzle with sesame oil and sprinkle with sesame seeds, if using. Serve while still warm. Leftovers will keep in a covered container in the refrigerator for up to 2 days.

Umami

Umami, often referred to as the fifth taste after sweet, sour, salty, and bitter, is central to Buddhist cooking in Japan, especially in the Shōjin Ryōri tradition (see page 92). It is characterized by a deep, rich, and savory flavor that lingers on the palate, promoting a sense of satisfaction and fullness. Ingredients rich in umami, like soy sauce, miso, seaweed, and mushrooms, are staples in Buddhist temple cuisine.

In Shōjin Ryōri, the subtle art of coaxing umami from vegetarian ingredients highlights the inherent flavors of nature without the use of animal products, aligning with Buddhist principles of nonviolence and respect for all life. Ingredients are treated with care and precision, through simmering, fermenting, and seasoning, to enhance their natural umami.

The experience of umami is an integral part of the mindfulness encouraged by Buddhism. It extends the act of eating beyond mere sustenance, turning it into a joyful appreciation of the richness and depth of flavors nature so generously provides.

Jackfruit Curry

PALĀ KORMA

SRI LANKA

SERVES 4

Embodying the vibrant colors and flavors of Sri Lanka, palā korma is an integral part of its culinary canvas. This aromatic, coconut-based curry has its origins in the Mughlai cuisine of the Indian subcontinent. Over the centuries, korma has evolved to accommodate local tastes and readily available seasonal ingredients, such as jackfruit, resulting in unique regional variations.

While Buddhist monks often eschew strong-smelling ingredients such as onions, garlic, and ginger (see page 29), this recipe calls for them, reflecting the dynamic dishes of Sri Lanka that burst with layers of potent flavors.

---

2 tablespoons vegetable oil

1 white onion, finely chopped

4 cloves garlic, minced

1 inch (2.5 cm) piece fresh ginger, peeled and minced

1 tablespoon ground coriander

1 tablespoon ground cumin

1 tablespoon ground turmeric

1 teaspoon red chile powder, such as Kashmiri

1 large carrot, finely chopped

2 cans (8 oz/225 g) jackfruit, coarsely chopped, or 1 large fresh jackfruit (see sidebar)

1 cup (90 g) green beans, cut into bite-size pieces

1 can (14 oz/400 g) coconut milk

Salt

Fresh cilantro leaves, for serving

Cooked rice, for serving

Naan, for serving (optional)

In a pan, heat the oil over medium heat. Add the onion, garlic, and ginger and sauté until aromatic and the onion turns translucent, about 7 minutes. Stir in the coriander, cumin, turmeric, and red chile powder and sauté for 2 minutes longer. Add the carrot and jackfruit and sauté for 5 minutes longer. Add the green beans and sauté until tender, about 3 minutes longer. Pour in the coconut milk, gently stirring until it is incorporated.

Reduce the heat to low, cover the pan, and gently simmer for 20 minutes, stirring every few minutes to prevent scorching and adding water, 2 tablespoons at a time, if the liquid is being absorbed too quickly. Remove from the heat and season to taste with salt. Spoon the korma into warm bowls, garnish with cilantro, and serve with rice and naan, if desired, alongside.

Preparing Fresh Jackfruit

Chopping fresh jackfruit can be a sticky process due to its natural latex content, but with a few steps, you can avoid a mess. Start by laying parchment on a work surface. Carefully oil a large, sharp knife blade to prevent the fruit from sticking to it.

Stand the jackfruit on one end and slice off the top and bottom to create a flat base. Starting at the top, use the knife to make shallow cuts into the skin, following the contours of the fruit and working your way down to its base. As you make the cuts, peel away the skin; this can be quite thick in some places, so ensure you cut deep enough to remove the entire green outer layer.

Next, cut the jackfruit into quarters or sections lengthwise. Inside each section, there will be yellow fruit pods surrounded by a fibrous interior.

Using your hands or the knife, gently extract the yellow pods, which contain the edible fruit. Pop out the seed inside each pod and discard it or save the seeds to cook later (they are edible when boiled or roasted). Once you've removed all the pods, slice or cut the jackfruit into bite-size pieces. It's now ready to be eaten fresh or used in various recipes. Be sure to clean up your work space immediately after preparing the jackfruit. Its latex is sticky and might leave residue on your knife and work surface. Clean your knife and any utensils immediately with hot soapy water. The fibrous parts of the jackfruit can be cooked to resemble pulled pork in texture.

SUSTAINABILITY

Buddhist monks embrace an abiding respect for the concept of sustainability, recognizing its significance in promoting balance and well-being for their bodies, their communities, and the planet. In the words of the British environmentalist Robert Swan, "The greatest threat to our planet is the belief that someone else will save it." This sentiment encapsulates the essence of temple cuisine, where monks actively take responsibility for their impact on the earth and prioritize sustainable practices in every aspect of their culinary journey.

At the monasteries, sustainability is ingrained in the way food is grown and cultivated. Monks practice mindful agriculture, adopting organic and regenerative farming methods that promote soil health and biodiversity. The practice of seed saving preserves heirloom varieties, ensuring genetic diversity and resilience in the crops they grow. The cultivation of seasonal produce further aligns with nature's cycles, reducing the need for artificial inputs and enhancing the nutritional value of their meals.

Food waste is considered a profound concern in temple cuisine. Monks adhere to the principle of non-wasting, ensuring that every part of an ingredient is used to its fullest extent and what cannot be used is either fed to birds or animals or composted to enrich the soil later on. Leftovers are honored and repurposed, reflecting the deep respect for the resources and efforts that go into food production.

Scientific research consistently reinforces the importance of sustainability in our food practices. Embracing sustainable growing, food preparation, and dining practices not only benefits the environment but also significantly enhances our health and mental well-being. Sustainable agriculture is known to yield more nutrient-dense and flavorful produce, contributing to improved physical health. The act of mindfully preparing and savoring sustainable meals fosters a deeper connection with our food and a sense of gratitude for the nourishment we receive and for the people who cultivate our food.

Beyond the individual benefits, incorporating sustainability into our daily lives also nurtures our relationships, our communities, and the environment. By mirroring Buddhist monks and engaging in practices that support ecological balance, we contribute to a healthier planet for future generations. Being mindful about sustainability can also alleviate the eco-anxiety many of us are experiencing today, empowering us to take tangible action and participate in creating a more sustainable world.

Practicing sustainability in our modern lives is attainable and rewarding. We can adopt regenerative gardening practices in our own backyards, support local farmers and artisans who prioritize sustainability, and mindfully use ingredients to minimize waste. By making small but meaningful changes, we can foster a more sustainable approach to food and cultivate a sense of harmony within ourselves and the world around us. It is also a wonderful example to set for our children, who will inherit this planet one day soon.

At its heart, sustainability is not just an ecological practice; it is a spiritual path that encourages us to live in harmony with the earth and with one another, just as monks do in temples throughout the world. As we embrace the timeless wisdom of temple cuisine, let us be inspired by the monks' dedication to sustainability, finding profound meaning and agency in the mindful cultivation, preparation, and enjoyment of food while improving our natural world at the same time.

Cauliflower Fried Rice

SERVES 4

Fried rice is a culinary staple in Chinese cuisine, and for many home cooks and Buddhist monks it embodies the philosophy of sustainability. This recipe mirrors the sustainable ethos by integrating cauliflower greens, alongside other components like the white parts of the celery and the cauliflower stalk. Embracing the zero-waste approach can yield delicious and creative meals that make the most out of what the earth so generously offers us.

Fried rice is a perfect canvas for using ingredients that might otherwise be discarded. It truly does embody the notion of using everything at our disposal. The stalks of broccoli, the tops of beets and carrots, and the stems of herbs can be chopped up and sautéed into the mix. The tough ends of asparagus can also be finely diced and added. Leftover rice from a previous meal finds new life in this dish. Even vegetable peels, rich in nutrients, can be incorporated after a good wash and some diligent chopping. By transforming these often-overlooked elements into a flavorful and filling meal, fried rice becomes not only a recipe but also a testament to sustainable cooking practices.

1 small head cauliflower

2 tablespoons toasted sesame oil

4 cups (620 g) cooked rice

2 ribs celery, thinly sliced

2 cups (180 g) finely shredded napa cabbage

1 cup (90 g) snow pea pods

2 tablespoons rice vinegar

2 tablespoons low-sodium soy sauce

1 teaspoon ground white pepper

Toasted white sesame seeds, for garnish

Rinse the cauliflower under cold running water to remove debris. Remove the leaves and thinly slice. Remove the florets and stem and coarsely chop. Heat the oil in a wok over medium-high heat. Add the rice, cauliflower florets and stem, and celery and stir-fry until the vegetables are tender-crisp, about 5 minutes. Add the cabbage and cauliflower leaves and stir-fry until the rice becomes slightly crispy, about 10 minutes. Add the snow pea pods, rice vinegar, soy sauce, and white pepper and stir-fry for 5 minutes longer. Distribute among warm bowls, sprinkle with sesame seeds, and serve. The rice will keep in a covered container in the refrigerator for up to 2 days.

Food Waste Meets Fried Rice

Using food waste in our daily meals is an innovative and empowering approach to sustainability, helping reduce our carbon footprint and promoting a zero-waste lifestyle. Incorporating these often-discarded items into plant-based fried rice not only elevates the dish's nutritional value but also imparts unique flavors and textures, making for a delightful and eco-friendly meal. Here are plant-based fried rice suggestions that incorporate elements typically considered food waste:

Stem Fried Rice
Use broccoli stems, cauliflower stems, or Swiss chard stems, finely chopped and sautéed until tender.

Leafy Greens Fried Rice
Incorporate the often-discarded outer leaves of lettuce, cabbage, or brussels sprouts, shredded and sautéed.

Root Peels Fried Rice
Collect and clean the peels from carrots, potatoes, or parsnips, ensuring they are pesticide-free. Thinly slice and sauté for added texture.

Corncob Fried Rice
After removing the kernels for other dishes, simmer corncobs in water to extract flavor and use that broth to cook rice. Dice any remaining kernels and toss them into the pan.

Sprouted Bean Fried Rice
If you have beans that have unintentionally sprouted, use them! They add a unique crunch and are nutritionally dense.

Pickle Brine Fried Rice
Instead of soy sauce, stir in a bit of pickle brine for tang and seasoning, using any pickled veggies in the mix.

Overripe Tomato Fried Rice
Dice overripe tomatoes and fold them into the rice, allowing their juices to add flavor and moisture.

Bread Crumb Fried Rice
Leftover or stale bread can be blitzed into crumbs and toasted with the rice for an added crunch.

Olive Brine Fried Rice
For a Mediterranean twist, use the brine from olives or capers as a seasoning agent.

Pumpkin Seed Husk Fried Rice
If you have pumpkin seed husks, toast them and sprinkle on top for added texture.

Fruit Scrap Fried Rice
Pineapple cores, apple peels, or the zest of citrus fruits (like orange or lemon) can be finely chopped and integrated for a sweet contrast.

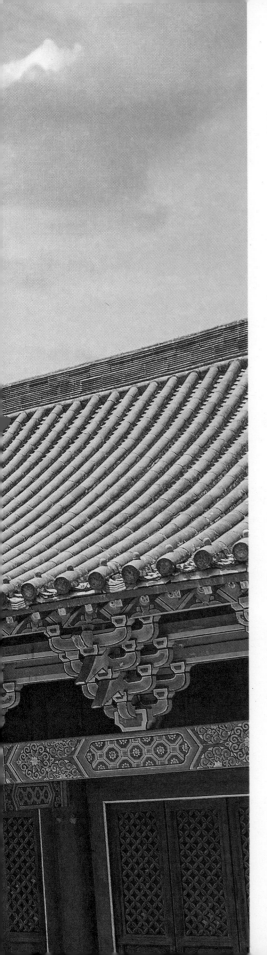

Shaolin Temple

China

Steeped in history and spirituality, the Shaolin Temple, located in the Songshan Mountain region of Henan Province, China, is an important bastion of Buddhist philosophy, martial arts, and vegetarian cuisine. As the birthplace of Chan Buddhism and Shaolin kung fu, the temple, founded in the 5th century CE, maintains a vibrant monastic life focused on discipline, mindfulness, and a sustainable lifestyle.

In the temple's kitchen, or jiào, the Shaolin monks prepare simple yet nourishing vegetarian dishes reflecting the principles of Buddhist cuisine. Staples include flavorful stir-fried vegetables, tofu dishes, rice, and fortifying noodle soups, made with local ingredients that are consumed in a reverent and grateful manner, reflecting the monks' commitment to sustainability and minimizing waste as a way to honor the earth that nourishes them.

The temple itself is a serene complex of traditional Chinese architecture that maintains the mystery and intrigue that the Shaolin monks are historically shrouded in, from ornate halls and soaring pagodas to a famed forest dense with ginkgo, cypress, maple, and pine trees that provide cover for funerary monuments known as steles. The monastery offers vegetarian meals to visitors, allowing them to partake in their sustainable dining practices that fuel the monks' intense martial arts sessions, which take place throughout the day.

The legendary Shaolin monks follow strict daily routines encompassing meditation, scripture studies, and martial arts training. Their customs echo their ascetic lifestyle and disciplined approach to both mind and body, personifying Buddhism's resilience and adaptability.

In their holistic approach to life, the Shaolin monks offer profound insights into harmonious living and sustainable practices, both in the kitchen and beyond. Their reverence for life translates into their culinary traditions, inviting us to explore the deeper connections between food, spirituality, and the preservation of our planet.

Spicy Fried Tempeh

SERVES 4

Sambal goreng tempeh is a lovely embodiment of the Buddhist commitment to sustainability. It includes tempeh, a fermented soybean product, effectively showcasing the Buddhist principle of turning simple, earth-friendly ingredients into delicious, nourishing meals. Buddhist monks in Indonesia embrace this dish, since tempeh is a rich protein source, a critical nutrient that is often challenging to integrate adequately into plant-based diets. The use of soybeans, a legume that replenishes the soil it grows in, embodies the Buddhist commitment to life's cyclical nature and sustainability.

There are many variations to sambal goreng tempeh, particularly in the type of sambal used. Sambal is a spicy chile-based condiment or sauce that is widely popular in Indonesia, Malaysia, Singapore, the southern Philippines, and other Southeast Asian countries. It's a versatile element in many dishes and can also be served as a side to enhance the flavors of meals.

---

2 tablespoons vegetable oil

¾ lb (340 g) tempeh, cut into 12 pieces

4 Roma tomatoes, coarsely chopped

2 red chiles, thinly sliced

2 green onions, thinly sliced

2 tablespoons tamarind paste

1½ tablespoons vegan fish sauce

1 tablespoon dark brown sugar

⅔ cup (180 ml) water

Fresh cilantro leaves, for garnish

Cooked rice, for serving (optional)

Line a plate with paper towels. Heat the oil in a pan over medium-high heat and fry the tempeh until it turns golden brown, about 3 minutes per side, flipping once using tongs. Transfer the tempeh to the plate to drain. Add the tomatoes, chiles, and green onions to the pan and sauté until tender and aromatic, about 3 minutes.

In a small bowl, whisk together the tamarind paste, fish sauce, dark brown sugar, and water until the sugar is dissolved and stir into the pan. Add the tempeh and spoon the sauce over it. Reduce the heat to low and gently simmer until the tempeh has absorbed the sauce and the flavors have had an opportunity to mingle, about 10 minutes. If the sauce becomes too thick during this step, add water, 1 tablespoon at a time, to loosen it up. Remove from the heat and transfer to warm plates. Garnish with cilantro and serve with rice, if desired. The tempeh will keep in a covered container in the refrigerator for up to 3 days.

Shaolin Martial Arts

A Tapestry of Spirituality and Discipline

Shaolin martial arts, often simply referred to as "Shaolin kung fu," are inextricably linked to the Buddhist monks of the Shaolin Temple (see page 115). Established in the dense forests of the Songshan Mountain range in China, this temple became the cradle for a unique blend of martial arts prowess and spiritual depth. The monks, in their pursuit of physical and mental discipline, developed these martial arts techniques not just as methods of self-defense, but as an extension of their Buddhist practices.

Buddhism, at its core, emphasizes the principles of mindfulness and meditation. The intricate movements of Shaolin martial arts require a heightened sense of awareness and focus, making them a physical manifestation of mindfulness. Each movement, each stance, demands the practitioner to be wholly present in the moment, echoing the teachings of Buddhism.

Meditation is a fundamental cornerstone of both Buddhism and Shaolin practices. For the monks, meditation is not just a means to spiritual enlightenment but also a way to refine their martial arts skills. The deep, introspective states achieved through meditation enable them to master complex techniques, harness their inner energy (chi), and react with precision. Shaolin martial arts are a seamless confluence of physical agility and spiritual depth, symbolizing the harmony between body and mind espoused by Buddhist teachings.

Pulled Noodle Soup

SERVES 4

Ramen, the beloved noodle soup of Japan, stands as a testament to the Buddhist philosophy of sustainability. While the origin of ramen is a bit contested, it is generally believed to have been introduced to Japan from China. The term *ramen* is the Japanese pronunciation of the Chinese characters "拉麵" (lā miàn), meaning "pulled noodles."

This recipe calls for shiitake powder, which can be found at Asian specialty markets. It's an umami bomb (see page 105) that monks in Japan add to many of their dishes for the protein and deep, unctuous flavor it offers. To make your own, see the recipe on the following page.

1 package (12 oz/340 g) ramen noodles

4 cups (960 ml) low-sodium vegetable broth

1 cup (240 ml) dashi

1 can (6 oz/170 g) bamboo shoots or 6 oz (170 g) thinly sliced fresh bamboo shoots

2 cups (180 g) fresh shiitake mushrooms, thinly sliced

1 cup (70 g) thinly sliced bok choy, equal parts leaves and stem

1 tablespoon white miso paste

1 tablespoon shiitake mushroom powder

2 tablespoons toasted sesame oil

2 tablespoons rice vinegar

1 package (12 oz/340 g) tempeh, sliced into 12 pieces

White sesame seeds, for garnish

Low-sodium soy sauce, for serving

To prepare the ramen, cook the ramen noodles according to the package instructions. Reserve 1 cup (240 ml) of the liquid and then drain the ramen in a colander. Rinse under cold running water to stop the cooking process. In a pot, combine the reserved ramen liquid, vegetable broth, and dashi and bring to a vigorous simmer over medium-high heat. Reduce the heat to medium and add the bamboo shoots, fresh shiitake mushrooms, and bok choy. Simmer until the bamboo and shiitakes are tender, about 5 minutes.

In a small bowl, combine ¼ cup (60 ml) of the ramen broth, the miso, and the shiitake mushroom powder and stir vigorously with a fork until incorporated. Stir this into the ramen broth along with 1 tablespoon of the sesame oil and 1 tablespoon of the vinegar. Reduce the heat to low and gently simmer for 15 minutes to enable the flavors to meld.

While the ramen broth simmers, in a pan, heat the remaining 1 tablespoon of sesame oil over medium heat. Add the tempeh and fry until golden brown on both sides, flipping once during the process, about 3 minutes per side.

Divide the ramen noodles among warm bowls. Ladle the ramen broth and vegetables on top and arrange a few slices of tempeh in the bowl. Garnish with sesame seeds and serve with soy sauce on the side. The ramen will keep in a covered container in the refrigerator for up to 3 days.

Shiitake Powder

Shiitake power adds an incredibly rich layer of meaty flavor and also imparts a silken texture to ramen. You'll want to keep it on hand as a secret taste enhancer. Sprinkle shiitake powder into soups, stir-fries, or even salad dressings to add a rich, earthy flavor. A little goes a long way, so start with a small amount and adjust according to taste.

¼ lb (115 g) dried shiitake mushrooms

Rub any excess debris from the shiitakes using a dry kitchen towel. Using a sharp knife, cut the mushrooms into fine pieces. Using a spice grinder, a food processor, or a mortar and pestle, grind the dried shiitakes as finely as you can. For a more uniform powder, sift through a fine-mesh sieve. Reserve the larger pieces for future use. The shiitake powder will keep in a dry, tightly sealed container at room temperature for at least 1 month.

More Ramen Ideas

Tofu: A different protein source that can be pan-fried or simmered in the broth.

Seaweed: Offers a depth of flavor to the broth and extra nutrients.

Sweet Corn: Adds a sweet crunch.

Bean Sprouts: Provide a fresh, crunchy texture.

Lotus Root: Thinly sliced and boiled or pan-fried, adds a unique texture and subtle flavor.

Tempura Vegetables: You can make a batter without eggs and use it to coat slices of vegetables like bell peppers, zucchini, or sweet potatoes. Fry them until crispy and add for an indulgent touch.

Additional Notes on Ramen

Japanese pulled noodles are produced using a technique of hand-stretching and pulling dough, rather than cutting or extruding it through machines. The most famous of the pulled noodles in Japanese cuisine is udon, though the traditional method of making udon does not typically involve the same kind of pulling technique seen in Chinese lā miàn or Korean kalguksu. In China, the art of noodle-pulling for lā miàn is a revered skill that requires significant practice to master. The dough is repeatedly stretched and folded upon itself to produce multiple strands of thin, even noodles. This mesmerizing process is both culinary art and entertainment, often showcased in restaurants and also mastered by Japanese and Chinese monks, who appreciate the routine and ritual of noodle-pulling, a meditative practice that requires the cook to remain present and fully immersed in the moment.

Over the past few decades, ramen has become a dish of the world. It has transcended its cultural origins and is warmly embraced by cultures all around the globe. From the bustling streets of Tokyo to the busy avenues of New York City, the appeal of this savory noodle dish is ubiquitous. Its flexible nature lends itself to countless regional variations and interpretations, enabling chefs and home cooks worldwide to infuse their own unique flavors and ingredients into the broth and toppings. Whether it's a simple bowl of instant noodles savored by a college student or an artisanal masterpiece crafted by a seasoned chef, ramen resonates with diverse communities as a comforting, flavorful, and often affordable meal. Its global popularity stands as testament to the universal language of good food and the joy it brings to tables everywhere.

Ramen is inherently adaptable, resonating with the Buddhist understanding of impermanence and adaptability. Buddhist monks in Japan appreciate ramen for its embodiment of the principle of interconnectedness. Every component of the dish, from the noodles to the broth, the tare (seasoning) to the toppings, has a vital role to play. Each ingredient contributes its flavors and textures to create a harmonious bowl of soup, illustrating how individual elements can come together to form a unified, delicious whole. The plant-based ramen recipe featured in this book celebrates these values, using a variety of vegetables, protein-rich tempeh, and flavorful broth. It illustrates the limitless possibilities of plant-based cooking and how sustainability and flavor can go hand in hand.

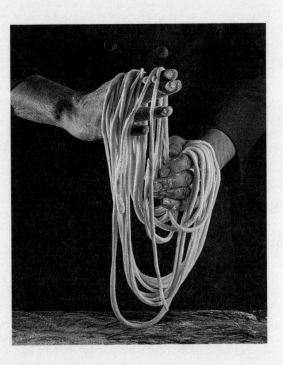

How to Introduce Sustainable Monastic Principles into Your Kitchen

In the hustle and bustle of our busy modern lives where we are being pulled in several directions all at once, adopting sustainable practices in our kitchens can seem daunting when measured against a never-ending to-do list. But through the lens of Buddhist principles, we can approach sustainability as a spiritual practice that nurtures both our bodies and the earth until its principles are innately stitched into the fabric of our days.

Minimizing food waste is a key aspect of a homegrown sustainable philosophy. Plan meals thoughtfully, don't buy fresh produce in excess, and use leftovers creatively to respect the labor and resources that bring food to our tables. This mindful consumption of the earth's resources reflects the Buddhist practice of mindfulness and gratitude.

Composting kitchen scraps transforms waste into nutrient-rich soil, embodying the Buddhist principle of interconnectedness and the cyclical nature of life. It's a practical, earth-friendly method that turns peels, coffee grounds, and vegetable trimmings into a gardener's gold, even if your garden consists of a windowsill herb planter in your studio apartment.

Eating seasonally and locally supports farmers, dials you into the harmonious rhythm of nature, and reduces the environmental impact of transportation, echoing the Buddhist respect for all life forms and our shared responsibility to protect the planet. Adopting a plant-based diet also significantly reduces water usage and greenhouse gas emissions, aligning with the Buddhist principle of ahimsa.

Practicing mindfulness while cooking and eating transforms these daily sustainable activities into enriching and meditative practices, fostering a deeper appreciation for food and its role in sustaining life. Inviting these behaviors into our kitchens not only leads to a more sustainable lifestyle, but also infuses everyday cooking and eating with a sense of purpose, joyfulness, and connection, making them feel deeply nourishing and satisfying.

Braised Baby Potatoes

SERVES 4

Algamja jorim is a popular Korean side dish known for its pleasurable blend of sweet and savory flavors. Korean Buddhist monks appreciate algamja jorim for its simple yet satisfying flavors and the way it embodies the Buddhist principle of sustainability, since it makes the most out of a humble, easily available ingredient—the potato.

Take your time braising the potatoes, washing them every few minutes with a spoonful of velvety sauce to enable them to slowly absorb the flavors. The patience and time braising requires reminds us to slow down, savor the present, and witness how a slow and steady routine that isn't rushed yields a rewarding result. Enjoy your algamja jorim as a side dish or with a bowl of warm rice.

---

1 lb (450 g) baby potatoes, rinsed well under cold water to remove excess residue

2 tablespoons toasted sesame oil

1½ cups (360 ml) water

2 tablespoons low–sodium soy sauce

2 tablespoons dark brown sugar

1 tablespoon cornstarch

Toasted white sesame seeds, for garnish

Cooked rice, for serving (optional)

Bring a pot of salted water to a boil over high heat. Add the potatoes, reduce the heat to medium, and simmer until the potatoes are just tender but still quite firm (they will finish cooking during the braising process; this step just helps get them started), 5 minutes. Drain and pat dry with a kitchen towel. In a pan, heat the sesame oil over medium heat. Add the potatoes and sauté until the skins begin to turn a light golden brown, turning a few times to ensure even cooking, about 5 minutes.

While the potatoes cook, in a bowl, whisk together the water, soy sauce, dark brown sugar, and cornstarch until the cornstarch is dissolved. Reduce the heat to low and pour the braising liquid over the potatoes, spooning it over them to ensure they are thoroughly enrobed. Cover the pan and braise until the potatoes are tender and the sauce is thickened and silky, about 15 minutes. Every 5 minutes or so, turn the potatoes over and spoon over the sauce to ensure even cooking. Transfer the potatoes to a serving platter using a slotted spoon, pour the braising liquid on top, and sprinkle with sesame seeds. Serve while still hot with a bowl of rice, if desired. The potatoes will keep in a covered container in the refrigerator for up to 3 days.

Chickpea Cakes

SERVES 6

Dhokla, a light and airy steamed chickpea cake from the state of Gujarat, is packed full of flavor, and its sunny yellow color is a lovely metaphor for India's vibrant culinary scene. Buddhist monks appreciate dhokla for its simple ingredients, gentle flavors, easily digestible ingredients, and the fact that it fits so well into their plant-based lifestyle. The foundation for dhokla is besan, also known as gram flour or chickpea flour. It's naturally gluten-free, high in protein, and has a slightly nutty flavor, which offers depth to the recipes in which it's used. Besan is widely available at Asian specialty markets.

1 cup (115 g) besan

1 cup (240 g) plain plant-based yogurt

1 tablespoon freshly squeezed lemon juice

2 teaspoons sugar

1 teaspoon salt

½ cup (120 ml) water, plus water as needed

1 teaspoon eno (see page 130)

1 tablespoon vegetable oil

1 teaspoon black mustard seeds

1 green chile, seeded and finely chopped

Grated coconut, for garnish

Fresh cilantro leaves, for garnish

In a large bowl, stir together the besan, plant-based yogurt, lemon juice, sugar, and salt. Mix well until everything is incorporated. Slowly add the water in a steady stream while stirring to form a batter similar to a pancake batter. If the batter is too thick, add a little more water, 1 tablespoon at a time, to achieve the desired result. Let the batter rest at room temperature for 15 minutes. Prepare the steamer as instructed on page 130 and lightly grease a 9 x 9-inch (23 x 23-cm) steaming dish with vegetable oil. Stir in the eno (or the substitute) and pour the batter into the steaming dish. Steam the batter according to the instructions on page 130 for 15–20 minutes, or until a toothpick inserted into the center comes out clean. Remove the dish from the steamer and let the dhokla rest at room temperature for at least 10 minutes.

While the dhokla cools, prepare the topping by heating the oil in a pan over medium heat. Add the mustard seeds and, once they start to pop, about 30 seconds, add the green chile and sauté until just tender, about 1 minute. Remove from the heat. Cut the dhokla into bite-size squares and arrange on a serving platter. Drizzle the topping over the dhokla and garnish with coconut flakes and cilantro. Serve immediately. The dhokla will keep in a covered container in the refrigerator for up to 3 days.

Additional Notes on Dhokla

Eno

This recipe calls for eno, also known as fruit salt in India, which is a quick-acting antacid comprising sodium bicarbonate, citric acid, and sodium carbonate—key effervescence-producing ingredients. It plays a vital role in dhokla by aiding in its fermentation, making the snack fluffy and light. Without eno, the dhokla may not rise as expected. If eno isn't available, an effective substitute could be a combination of baking soda and lemon juice or vinegar. The chemical reaction between the acid (lemon/vinegar) and the base (baking soda) mimics eno's effervescence, facilitating the rise and fluffiness of the dhokla. For 1 teaspoon of eno, you could substitute a combination of ½ teaspoon of baking soda and ½ teaspoon of lemon juice or vinegar. This mixture will create a similar effervescence and leavening effect in your dhokla. Regardless of whether you're using eno or a substitute, add it right before you're ready to steam the dhokla, as the reaction starts immediately.

Setting Up a Home Steamer for Dhokla

Dhokla is steamed, and while that might feel like a fussy measure, setting up a steamer for it involves a few simple steps. Be careful when using steam to avoid burns. Use oven mitts or tongs when handling hot dishes and keep your face and hands away from the pot when removing the lid, as a rush of hot steam will escape.

Choose a large deep pan or pot with a lid that fits securely. Pour 1–2 inches (2.5–5 cm) of water into the pot. The water level should be lower than your steaming plate's bottom when it's inserted into the pot (the food should not touch the water at all during steaming). Place a metal trivet or a heatproof stand such as an upside-down plate into the pot. This will hold the dish containing the dhokla batter above the water level. Make sure the stand is tall enough to keep your dhokla dish out of the water. If you don't have a steamer, you can use a regular cake pan or a deep dish that fits into your pot. Grease it lightly with oil to prevent sticking.

Pour the batter into the greased dish. Carefully place the filled dish on the stand in the pot. Cover the pot with the lid. It's important to have a tight seal for effective steaming, so make sure the lid fits well. Turn the heat to medium-high. Once the water starts boiling, reduce the heat to medium-low and let the dhokla steam. The cooking time will depend on the size of your dhokla dish and the thickness of the batter.

A Brief History of Dhokla (and Gujarat)

Dhokla is believed to have originated in Gujarat around the 7th century CE. Its popularity spread across India and today it is relished in homes, as a street food, and in restaurants and temples all over the country. This dhokla recipe is emblematic of the Buddhist ethos of sustainability, simplicity, and resourcefulness. Gujarat, a state on the western coastline of India, is widely recognized for its predominantly vegetarian cuisine, a dietary choice influenced by religious beliefs, culture, and lifestyle. A significant percentage of the population practices Jainism and Hinduism, religions that often advocate for a vegetarian diet due to principles of nonviolence and respect toward all forms of life. This is reflected in the local cuisine, which is renowned for its diverse and rich array of vegetarian dishes. Signature dishes like dhokla, khakhra (a thin, spiced wheat cracker), thepla (an aromatic bread), and undhiyu (a vegetable dish) are all vegetarian, often using pulses, grains, and a variety of local vegetables.

Gujarat's commitment to vegetarianism is such that it even passed legislation in 2011 strengthening laws against cow slaughter, underlining the cultural and religious significance of vegetarianism in the state.

Despite Gujarat not being widely recognized as a center for Buddhism, it houses a few significant Buddhist monuments and temples that highlight the spread of Buddhism during ancient times. One notable location is Devni Mori, a Buddhist archaeological site near Shamlaji in the Aravalli district of Gujarat, where remains of a Buddhist monastery and stupa from the 3rd–4th century CE have been unearthed. The most significant find from this site is a casket containing relics believed to be those of Buddha himself. In keeping with the Buddhist tradition of not disclosing the specific type of sacred relics discovered at burial sites, the nature of the relics has not been revealed.

Vegetarianism and Veganism

At the heart of Buddhist, Hindu, Sikh, Jain, and many other monastic culinary traditions lies a deep respect for all forms of life, often leading monks to adopt vegetarian or vegan diets. This principle of the Sanskrit word *ahimsa* (non-harm) nurtures a compassionate relationship with our environment and fellow beings, reinforcing a fulfilling and harmonious coexistence.

Vegetarian and vegan diets focus on plant-based ingredients such as grains, legumes, fruits, and vegetables. These are not only nutritionally rich ingredients, but their production also has a lower environmental impact compared to animal-based foods, aligning with Buddhism's teachings of interconnectedness and environmental stewardship.

Scientific studies affirm the health benefits of plant-based diets, including reduced risks of heart disease, diabetes, dementia, and certain cancers. Shifting toward such diets also significantly contributes to mitigating climate change by reducing greenhouse gas emissions and conserving water and land resources.

In Buddhism, the act of eating is not merely a biological function but also a spiritual practice. The principle of transference, where our actions can benefit all beings, aligns with a plant-based diet. By choosing not to harm animals or use their by-products for food, we can practice compassion and generate positive karma, which benefits ourselves and others.

Embracing a plant-based diet leads to improved physical health, mental clarity, and spiritual growth, fostering an attitude of gratitude and mindfulness toward food and the resplendent planet that provides it. It echoes the way Buddhist monks live— in harmony with themselves, each other, and the earth—and turns each meal into a celebration of life and interdependence.

Fried Potato Cakes

SERVES 4

Potato cakes, or perkedel, as they're known in Indonesia, are a widely loved part of the nation's culinary tapestry. These savory, golden-brown cakes have a crisp exterior and soft, flavorful interior. Despite the absence of onions, garlic, or ginger, which would typically be included in this recipe, this monastic-friendly version is just as delectable with its crunchy texture that gives way to a pillowy interior. Perkedel has a lacy coating that is traditionally achieved using an egg batter. For a plant-based alternative, this recipe uses a cornstarch slurry instead.

6 russet potatoes, quartered (reserve the peelings for vegetable broth or fried rice, or compost them)

1 tablespoon low-sodium soy sauce

Freshly ground black pepper

½ cup (120 ml) water

2 tablespoons cornstarch

Vegetable oil, for frying

Plant-based dipping sauce of choice, for serving

Bring a pot of salted water to a boil over high heat. Reduce the heat to medium, add the potatoes, and cook until easily pierced with a fork, about 20 minutes. Drain and cool the potatoes. Mash the potatoes using a potato masher or a fork until just smooth. Do not over-mash them or the starch will be overworked and they will become gummy. Stir the soy sauce into the potatoes and season to taste with pepper. By hand, or using a a 3-inch (7.5-cm) ring mold, shape the potatoes into cakes about 1 inch (2.5 cm) thick and 3 inches (7.5 cm) in diameter.

Combine the water and cornstarch in a small bowl and vigorously stir together with a fork until a slurry is formed. Line a plate with paper towels. Add 6 inches (15 cm) of oil to a heavy-bottom pot over high heat and heat until a drop of water flicked onto the surface of the oil sizzles. Dredge one of the perkedel in the cornstarch slurry and, using a slotted spoon or a spider, carefully place it in the hot oil and fry until it is light golden brown on all sides, gently turning it over in the oil a few times to ensure even cooking. Keep in mind that the perkedel will continue to cook after it is removed from the oil, so removing it when it is a light shade of golden brown is ideal. Repeat the process with the remaining perkedel. Serve while hot with a plant-based dipping sauce (opposite). Perkedel will keep in a covered container in the refrigerator for up to 2 days (although they won't be as crispy after they are chilled). Perkedel can be reheated, but refrying will cause them to become quite oily.

Plant-Based Dipping Sauces

Here are a few plant-based dipping sauces that you can serve with perkedel:

Sweet Soy Glaze
Combine equal parts soy sauce and brown sugar. Simmer until thickened.

Peanut Sauce
Blend roasted peanuts, soy sauce, coconut milk, lime juice, and a hint of brown sugar.

Chile-Tamarind Sauce
Blend tamarind paste, brown sugar, and a hint of chile paste.

Sesame-Tahini Sauce
Blend tahini, soy sauce, rice vinegar, and a sprinkle of toasted sesame seeds.

Coconut-Lime Sauce
Whisk together coconut milk, lime juice, soy sauce, and a sprinkle of brown sugar.

FLAVOR, COLOR & PRESERVATION

Color, food preservation, fermentation, and flavor are the essential elements that infuse monastic temple cuisine with unparalleled richness and depth, elevating the enjoyment and appreciation of every meal. These elements connect us to our recipes in ways that enliven all of our senses and take us on an enriching and exciting multisensory journey.

Buddhist monks deeply understand the importance of flavor, recognizing it as an integral part of temple cuisine and Buddhism. The wise and beloved Buddhist monk Thich Nhat Hanh once remarked, "Flavor is the substance of life; it brings joy and nourishment to both body and soul." This sentiment resonates with the essence of temple cuisine, where the artful balance of flavor elevates every dish into a culinary masterpiece, in spite of its simplicity, nourishing not only the body but also the spirit.

At Buddhist monasteries, food preservation techniques are also cherished and passed down through generations. Monks use traditional methods such as pickling, drying, and fermenting to preserve seasonal produce, ensuring a constant supply of nourishment throughout the year. Fermentation, in particular, adds depth and complexity to flavors, enhancing the taste and the nutritional value of ingredients.

The vibrant colors of temple cuisine also play a significant role in creating an enticing dining experience. Monks artfully combine a spectrum of shades, appealing to our innate senses and enhancing our enjoyment of the meal. This practice reflects the understanding that we eat with our eyes first, and color can deeply influence our dining experiences and even our memories.

Scientific research supports the value of food preservation, fermentation, flavor, and color in enhancing both physical and mental well-being. Fermented foods are known to be rich in probiotics, promoting gut health and overall digestion. Flavorful and radiantly colorful dishes can increase our satisfaction and satiety, leading to a more balanced and mindful approach to eating.

Keeping in mind these culinary practices as we cook and plate our food contributes to more memorable dining experiences, heightening the joy of celebrations and everyday moments, which in turn deepen our sense of connection to one another. The artful use of seasoning and flavor can turn a simple meal into a culinary adventure, creating lasting memories that we cherish for years to come.

The wisdom of temple cuisine can be easily incorporated into our daily lives. By exploring food preservation techniques, we can make the most of seasonal abundance and also reduce food waste. Experimenting with various herbs, spices, seasonings, and parts of ingredients we might normally discard can creatively elevate our home-cooked dishes and introduce new dimensions of flavor, color, and excitement.

In addition to enriching our dining experiences, being mindful about flavor can have positive impacts on our health and well-being. Choosing whole and flavorful ingredients can encourage us to eat more mindfully and savor each bite, promoting a more balanced and nourishing relationship with food. Embracing these tenets of Buddhist temple cuisine by inviting vibrant flavors, colors, fermented items, and artful presentations elevates our appreciation for the nourishment that sustains us.

Sweet and Sour Cabbage Pickles

SERVES 4

Dưa chua, Vietnamese sweet and sour pickled cabbage, embodies the ancient Buddhist practice of food preservation and the value monks place on sustainability. Hailing from Northern Vietnam, dưa chua has been a staple in Vietnamese cuisine for generations. Its refreshing sweetness and tanginess balance the richer, savory flavors of many traditional dishes. It can be used to garnish sandwiches or complement rice dishes, or be enjoyed on its own.

---

1 head napa cabbage, quartered, cored, and leaves finely shredded

2 tablespoons kosher salt

2 cups (480 ml) rice vinegar

2 cups (480 ml) water

2 tablespoons sugar

1 Thai red chile, thinly sliced (optional)

In a large bowl, toss together the cabbage and salt. Transfer to a colander set over a bowl and let drain for 1½ hours. This step enables the salt to leach as much liquid as possible from the cabbage to ensure that it remains crispy. With clean hands, firmly squeeze the cabbage to remove any residual liquid.

In a pot, bring the vinegar, water, and sugar to a simmer over medium heat. Continue to simmer until the sugar is dissolved, about 5 minutes. Place the cabbage and chile, if using, in a sterilized and heatproof jar with a latch and a firm seal. Pour the hot vinegar on top, making sure that it fills the entire jar and that everything is submerged. Let stand with the lid open until it has cooled. Latch the lid and refrigerate for at least a week to enable the cabbage to ferment. The pickles will keep in the refrigerator for about 3 weeks.

More Dưa Chua Ideas

The tangy nature of dưa chua can refresh and balance out many dishes, making it a versatile addition to various culinary creations.

Here are six more ways to use dưa chua to brighten your meals:

Bánh Mì Fillings
The crisp texture and tangy flavor of dưa chua make it a perfect addition to Vietnamese sandwiches or bánh mì (see page 190), complementing the other ingredients and adding a refreshing crunch.

Spring Rolls
Incorporate dưa chua in fresh spring rolls (see page 171) along with herbs, tofu, or shrimp for added flavor and texture.

Salads
Toss dưa chua into various salads to introduce a zesty element, balancing out sweeter or richer components.

Tofu or Tempeh Toppings
Sautéed tofu or tempeh can be garnished with dưa chua for a punchy, tangy contrast.

Grilled Vegetables
Serve dưa chua alongside grilled vegetables. Its refreshing tanginess can cut through the smokiness and richness of grilled dishes.

Noodle Bowls
Sprinkle dưa chua over noodle bowls or phở (see page 26) to add a crunchy, tangy dimension to the warm, comforting broth and noodles.

Truc Lam Temple

Vietnam

Situated amid the lush, tranquil highlands of Dalat in Vietnam, Truc Lam Temple and its monks breathe colorful life into the vivid culinary traditions of Buddhist temple cuisine. Adhering to a plant-based diet, the temple ensures that food preparation relies heavily on fermentation and preservation, mirroring Buddhist teachings of patience and sustainability. Ingredients such as tofu and seasonal vegetables are often fermented, introducing a distinctive palate of flavors and vibrant colors to monastic meals.

Mainstay dishes include dau hu chien sa ot, fragrant fried tofu with lemongrass and chile, and nom du du, a crunchy green papaya salad. Like most of the recipes at the Truc Lam Temple, they reflect the multisensory balance of flavor, color, texture, and aroma that is so integral to Vietnamese Buddhist cuisine.

The monastery is relatively new compared to others throughout Asia. It was founded in 1994 and overlooks the serene Tuyen Lam Lake, which provides an ideal setting for monks to practice their spiritual and dietary disciplines. This exquisite temple also stands as a beacon connecting the local community and visitors with the Buddhist monks who live there.

Truc Lam Temple not only offers the monks a spiritual refuge, but it also invites visitors to enjoy meals prepared by the monks, encapsulating the harmony of Buddhist teachings with everyday culinary practices. In Vietnam, Buddhism is entwined with everyday life, instilling mindfulness, gratitude, respect for nature, and the pursuit of inner tranquility—a philosophy that is tangibly evident in the temple's cuisine.

Vegetable Rice

SERVES 4

Bibimbap not only showcases the Buddhist value of appreciating the diversity of nature with its vibrant colors, contrasting textures, and variety of flavors, but also encapsulates the monastic ethos of simplicity and balance, eating in step with the seasons, and embracing a sustainable lifestyle. Each ingredient in the dish is treated with care and attention, a culinary manifestation of the Buddhist teaching of mindfulness.

1½ tablespoons toasted sesame oil

1 lb (450 g) wild mushrooms, cut into bite-size pieces

1 cup (110 g) finely grated carrots

1 zucchini, quartered and thinly sliced

1 cup (90 g) shredded napa cabbage

1 cup (90 g) coarsely chopped bok choy (white and green parts)

¾ cup (30 g) bean sprouts

1 cup (30 g) fresh baby spinach

2 tablespoons rice vinegar

1½ tablespoons low-sodium soy sauce, plus soy sauce for serving

4 cups cooked short-grain rice, for serving

Toasted white sesame seeds, for garnish

Gochujang, for serving

In a pan, heat the oil over medium heat, add the wild mushrooms, carrots, zucchini, and cabbage and sauté until the vegetables are tender, about 7 minutes. Add the bok choy, bean sprouts, spinach, and rice vinegar and sauté for 5 minutes longer. Stir in the soy sauce and remove from the heat.

To serve, distribute the rice into warm bowls, spoon the vegetables on top, and garnish with sesame seeds. Serve with soy sauce and gochujang on the side so each person can add as much heat as they prefer.

NOTE: Traditionally, the ingredients in bibimbap are cooked separately and then distributed individually in the bowl for a stunning presentation. In this recipe, the elements are cooked together in order to decrease the cooking time. Feel free to cook and arrange each item separately for a more traditional bibimbap experience.

More Bibimbap Ideas

Here are a few more ideas to add variety to your bibimbap:

Tofu Bibimbap
Add tofu for more texture and protein.

Tempeh Bibimbap
Use marinated and sautéed tempeh instead of tofu for a nutty, chewy protein source.

Kimchi Bibimbap
Add some vegan kimchi for an extra layer of flavor and a probiotic boost.

Seaweed Bibimbap
Sprinkle some shredded nori or crumbled gim (roasted seaweed) for a sea-salty touch.

Pickled Radish Bibimbap
Add some tanginess with slices of pickled radish (sòn lăbu; see page 150).

Avocado Bibimbap
Add avocado slices for a creamy, rich variation.

Additional Notes on Bibimbap

Bibimbap's origins trace back to the Joseon dynasty (1392–1910 CE). It was traditionally eaten on the eve of the Lunar New Year as a way to use up all the leftover side dishes before the start of a new year. Today, it is enjoyed year-round and has become a symbol of Korean culinary heritage.

The addition of mushrooms to this recipe reflects the value Korean monks place on this humble but umami-packed ingredient. In the tranquil mountains surrounding their temples, monks have long practiced the meditative art of foraging for wild mushrooms. This tradition, deeply embedded in Korean Buddhist culture, symbolizes the harmony between nature and spirituality. By sourcing their sustenance directly from the earth, the monks embody the Buddhist principles of presence and interconnectedness. Foraging requires patience, keen observation, and a profound respect for the environment—all core tenets of Buddhism. By consuming what nature offers, the monks embrace a diet that not only sustains their physical being but also nurtures their spiritual journey, reinforcing the cyclical bond between nature, nourishment, and enlightenment.

A famous Korean Buddhist nun, Jeong Kwan, who is known for her temple cuisine, once said, "There are boundaries in food. I've come out to the world so that I could interact with people about food and share my ideas with them." Bibimbap embodies this philosophy; it's comfort food that feeds the body, heart, and spirit and brings us all together.

The Interplay of Color, Meditation, and Culinary Artistry

In the realm of Buddhism, color is more than a mere sensory perception; it holds profound spiritual significance, particularly within meditation practices. The Theravada Buddhist tradition's meditation on *kasinas* illustrates this. A kasina is an object of focus, and some are based on colors like blue, yellow, or red. Practitioners use colored disks, immersing themselves in the hue, training the mind to achieve deep concentration and clarity.

This meditative focus on color is akin to the cook's palette. Just as meditation uses the kasina to engage the mind, chefs and home cooks can use vibrant and diverse colors in cuisine to evoke emotions, stimulate the senses, and tell stories. The plate becomes a canvas, each ingredient a brushstroke. Like the kasina meditator, the diner is invited to focus deeply, savoring each hue and flavor. The spiritual practice of color-based meditation finds a parallel in the culinary world, reminding us of the interconnectedness of all experiences.

Pickled Radishes

SERVES 4

Buddhist traditions in Tibet have been shaped and hardened by geopolitical struggle. In spite of centuries of hardship born of a perpetual battle for survival and an enduring commitment to maintaining autonomy, Buddhist monks continue to not only survive but also thrive, radiating wisdom, resilience, and a deep respect for life and, in turn, cultivating deep and abiding respect from their communities. One of the most poignant expressions of this enduring spirit is found in the Tibetan kitchen, with its emphasis on simplicity, resourcefulness, and sustainability. Sòn lābu, a traditional Tibetan preparation of fermented radish, embodies this ethos.

1 large daikon, quartered and thinly sliced

2 bunches red radishes, thinly sliced (reserve the radish tops for another use)

½ cup (80 g) kosher salt

2 cups (480 ml) white vinegar

2 cups (480 ml) water

4 Thai red chiles, thinly sliced

3 inches (7.5 cm) fresh ginger, peeled and thinly sliced

1 tablespoon Sichuan peppercorns (or black peppercorns)

In a large bowl, toss together the daikon and red radishes with the salt. Transfer to a colander set over a bowl and let drain for 1½ hours. This step enables the salt to leach as much liquid as possible from the radishes to ensure that they remain crispy. With clean hands, gently squeeze the radishes to remove any residual liquid. In a pot, combine the vinegar and water and bring to a simmer over medium-high heat. Into a sterilized and heatproof container with a latch and a firm seal, spoon about a quarter of the radishes and then sprinkle with a quarter each of the chile slices, ginger, and peppercorns. Spoon another layer of radishes and top with another layer of aromatics. Continue with the remaining ingredients. Pour the hot vinegar on top, making sure that it fills the entire jar and that everything is submerged. Let stand with the lid open until it has cooled. Latch the lid and refrigerate for at least a week to enable the radishes to ferment. They will keep in the refrigerator for about 3 weeks.

More Sòn Lābu Ideas

Sòn lābu, with its tangy, crisp taste, can be used as a versatile accompaniment in many meals. Here are some suggestions:

With Steamed Rice
Sòn lābu can be served alongside steamed rice, adding a burst of flavor to this staple dish.

In Sandwiches or Wraps
It can be used as a filling in sandwiches or wraps, much like pickles, to provide a crunchy, sour note.

As a Side with Curries or Stews
The crisp, sour taste of the fermented radish can offset the richness of curries or stews and add complexity to their flavor profile.

In Salads
Sòn lābu can be mixed into salads to add an extra layer of taste and texture.

With Noodles
Whether it's rice noodles, udon, or soba, a side of sòn lābu can add a pleasant tanginess to these dishes.

With Tibetan Bread (Balep Korkun)
Sòn lābu and a piece of Tibetan bread can make for a simple and satisfying snack or meal.

In Stir-Fries
Sòn lābu can be added to stir-fries for a zingy flavor. Remember to add it toward the end of cooking to maintain its crunch.

With Momos (Tibetan Dumplings)
Traditionally served with a fiery tomato chutney, momos can also be complemented by the tangy sòn lābu.

Remember, the joy of cooking lies in experimentation! Feel free to try sòn lābu with your favorite dishes and explore new combinations.

Additional Notes on Sòn Lābu

This recipe includes the intriguing Sichuan peppercorn, a unique seasoning native to China but also common in Tibet. Unlike typical peppercorns, the Sichuan peppercorn imparts a tingling, almost numbing sensation on the palate, elevating the dish with its distinctive citrusy flavor. Beyond its zesty taste, this peppercorn embodies an all-encompassing sensory experience, invigorating dishes with an aromatic complexity and a sensation that dances on the tongue, making it a standout ingredient in any culinary creation. It's not a necessary addition for this recipe, but if you are able to source Sichuan peppercorns, they add a fun and uplifting zing. If you are not able to source them, black peppercorns are a fine substitute.

Fermentation and Food Preservation

Fermentation and food preservation form the lifeblood of many Asian temple cuisines, resonating with the fundamental Buddhist philosophy of sustainability and balance. The vibrant and bright flavors of fermented foods also enliven the palate, reminding us to be more present in our food consumption. Revered for their health benefits and potential to reduce waste and increase self-sufficiency, preservation traditions are deeply embedded in monastic dietary principles.

Buddha emphasized the importance of mindful eating, and fermentation is a practice that embodies this lesson. It transforms raw ingredients into nutrient-rich foods like kimchi, sòn lābu, and miso. All of these products are packed with probiotics that are beneficial for gut health (which many scientists say also contributes to mental clarity and brain health). The preservation process, whether through salt, vinegar or another acid, soy sauce, or dehydration, amplifies the flavors of ingredients, making meals more dynamic and satisfying.

Food preservation techniques also align with Buddha's teachings about appreciating and using all available resources, aiding the fight against food waste. A carrot top, instead of being discarded, can be pickled or dehydrated, magically transforming it into a tasty, nutritious condiment.

Introducing these techniques into the home kitchen can be a meaningful way to practice sustainability, while enhancing our meals with unique flavors and health benefits. By embracing these age-old methods, we align ourselves with the Buddhist belief in living harmoniously with nature, optimizing resources, and treating food as a source of nourishment for both body and spirit.

LARB JAY
THAILAND

Vegetable Salad

SERVES 4

Larb, a flavor-packed meat salad that is often regarded as the national dish of Laos, also enjoys immense popularity in Thailand, especially in the northeastern region, known as Isan. Larb jay or vegetarian larb is a plant-based version of this dish, embodying the colors, textures, and tastes in a vibrant salad that is packed with flavor and nutritional benefits.

This recipe calls for khao khua, or roasted rice powder, which acts as a thickening agent for the tofu, imparting a silken texture and subtly nutty flavor. Khao khua is available at Asian specialty markets. If you can't find it, don't worry. Larb jay is just as delicious without it. Or if you would like to make your own, toast uncooked sticky rice in a dry pan until golden, let cool, and then grind into a coarse powder using a mortar and pestle or a spice grinder.

---

1 tablespoon vegetable oil

1 cup (225 g) crumbled firm tofu

1 cup (170 g) fresh corn kernels

½ cup (85 g) quartered cherry tomatoes

2 tablespoons khao khua

1 tablespoon low-sodium soy sauce

1 tablespoon vegan fish sauce

Juice of 2 limes

1 tablespoon dark brown sugar

¾ cup (100 g) sliced cucumbers

½ cup (15 g) loosely packed fresh mint leaves

½ cup (15 g) loosely packed fresh cilantro leaves

3 heads Little Gem lettuce, leaves separated

In a pan, heat the oil over medium heat. Add the tofu and sauté until it begins to turn golden brown, about 5 minutes. Add the corn kernels and sauté until they are slightly charred, about 10 minutes. Reduce the heat to low and stir in the tomatoes. Sauté until they begin to soften, about 3 minutes. In a small bowl, stir together the khao khua, soy sauce, fish sauce, lime juice, and dark brown sugar until incorporated. Stir into the pan and cook until the sauce begins to thicken, about 5 minutes. Remove from the heat and mix in the cucumbers, mint, and cilantro.

To serve, arrange the lettuce leaves on a serving platter and spoon the larb jay into them. Serve immediately. Larb jay doesn't keep very well because the ingredients will become soggy when refrigerated. It's best to enjoy right away!

Tofu

Tofu, also known as bean curd, is a versatile food derived from soybeans. It's available in various types and consistencies, which makes it suitable for a wide range of plant-based dishes, from savory to sweet. Different types of tofu are suitable for various dishes and culinary applications, so it's beneficial to choose the right type for each recipe to achieve the desired texture and flavor outcome.

Here are some common types of tofu:

Silken Tofu

This type has a creamy, custard-like texture and is usually used in desserts, smoothies, soups, or salad dressings.

Soft Tofu

Slightly firmer than silken but still delicate, soft tofu is often used in soups like miso or in gentle simmered dishes.

Medium-Firm Tofu

This has a denser texture than soft tofu but is not as hard as its firm counterparts. It can be crumbled and used in a variety of dishes.

Firm Tofu

This tofu holds its shape well, making it suitable for frying, sautéing, grilling, or stir-frying. It can be easily marinated because it absorbs flavors well.

Extra-Firm Tofu

With the least amount of moisture among the firm tofu varieties, extra-firm tofu has a very dense texture. It's ideal for grilling, stir-frying, or any cooking method that requires the tofu to maintain its shape.

Sprouted Tofu

Made from sprouted soybeans, this tofu is believed to be more nutritious and digestible than tofu made from non-sprouted soybeans. Its texture is similar to firm or extra-firm tofu.

Smoked Tofu

As the name suggests, this tofu has been smoked, providing it with a distinct flavor and darker outer layer. It's ready to eat out of the package and can be added to salads, sandwiches, or other dishes.

Fermented Tofu

This type of tofu undergoes fermentation, resulting in a strong flavor. There are various types of fermented tofu, such as stinky tofu and tofu cheese.

Tofu Skin (Yuba)

As soy milk is heated, a skin forms on its surface, which can be harvested as yuba. It can be used fresh or dried in various dishes, from soups to wraps.

Carrot Salad

SERVES 4

Danggeun muchim is a simple, yet delightful carrot salad from the culinary repertoire of Korea. Bursting with tantalizing flavor and vibrant color, it is a lovely representation of the Korean affection for fresh and colorful seasonal produce and an embodiment of Buddhist principles of mindful eating.

In Korean Buddhist monasteries, this dish fits naturally into a diet that respects the cycles of nature and the interconnectedness of all beings. Every ingredient at the temple, including the humble carrot, is treated with reverence and gratitude. It exemplifies the beauty of simplicity, as both an ingredient and in its preparation. The vibrant color of the carrots is an embodiment of the Buddhist nature: colorful, unpretentious, and nourishing. This simple dish not only highlights the natural sweetness and crunch of the carrots but also offers nutritional benefits. Carrots are rich in beta-carotene, a compound our body converts into vitamin A, essential for good vision, skin health, and robust immunity.

---

1 tablespoon sesame oil

1½ tablespoons rice vinegar

1 teaspoon sugar

½ teaspoon salt

4 large carrots, finely grated

1½ tablespoons toasted black sesame seeds

Cooked rice, for serving

In a small bowl, whisk together the sesame oil, vinegar, sugar, and salt until the sugar is dissolved. Place the carrots in a large bowl and stir in the dressing until the carrots are glistening. Garnish with the sesame seeds and serve in a communal bowl with rice on the side.

Flavor and Color

Flavor and color greatly enhance our culinary experience, weaving together a tempting tapestry that speaks to our senses and our emotions. In monastic temple cuisine, this mosaic of flavor and color is central to the mindfulness of meal preparation and consumption.

Buddhist wisdom emphasizes being present in each moment. Flavor, the intriguing balance of sweet, sour, salty, bitter, and umami (see page 105), demands our attention, inviting us to fully experience and fully savor each bite. The vibrant colors in temple cuisine serve a dual purpose: They reflect the seasonal and local produce of the region, echoing Buddhism's reverence for nature and the cyclical rhythm of life, and they act as a visual feast, stimulating our appetite even before the first bite. Thich Nhat Hanh, the revered Buddhist monk, has written about eating as an act of awakening, a process in which color and flavor play critical roles.

Bringing flavor and color into the meals we prepare in our home kitchens can enrich our meals, build stronger memories, and strengthen our connection to our food. Experiment with fresh herbs, spices, preserved items, and locally sourced ingredients to amplify flavor and color in your dishes. We eat with our eyes first. A visually appealing, colorful plate not only tempts the palate but also embodies the principle of harmony with nature and abiding appreciation for the present moment, a cornerstone of Buddhist philosophy.

Baked Vegetable Fritters

SERVES 6

Samosas are an integral part of Indian cuisine, with a rich history dating back centuries. Originating in West Asia, they were introduced to India by traders and have since become a beloved staple, with regional variations across the country. In the context of Buddhist philosophy, the making of samosas can be a practice of ritual and routine, as it involves a series of deliberate, thoughtful steps. The routine of preparing the dough, carefully crafting the filling, and forming the samosas can be a form of ritual that aligns with Buddhist principles.

Indian Buddhist monks, similar to their counterparts in other Buddhist traditions, eat simple foods and avoid ingredients considered to stimulate the senses excessively, such as onions and garlic. These vegetarian samosas, filled with humble, seasonal vegetables and subtle spices, fit into their dietary practices. The accompanying mint dipping sauce adds a refreshing contrast to the samosas, offering a complete taste experience of warmth from the samosas and coolness from the mint sauce. This balance aligns with the Buddhist philosophy of the Middle Way (see page 60), which advocates for a balanced approach to life.

FOR THE SAMOSA DOUGH

2 cups (230 g) all-purpose flour

1 teaspoon salt

½ cup (120 ml) vegetable oil

½ cup (120 ml) warm water

To prepare the samosa dough, mix the flour and salt together in a large bowl and then stir in the vegetable oil. Use your hands to bring the dough together and then add the water in a slow, steady stream while kneading until it resembles a shaggy ball. Cover the bowl with a damp kitchen towel and let it rest at room temperature for 30 minutes.

Recipe continues

FOR THE FILLING

1 tablespoon vegetable oil

1 teaspoon cumin seeds

2 carrots, finely chopped

2 cups (280 g) green peas

3 cups (120 g) coarsely chopped kale

1 teaspoon ground turmeric

1 teaspoon garam masala

½ cup (15 g) loosely packed torn fresh mint leaves

½ cup (15 g) loosely packed fresh cilantro leaves

Salt

FOR THE DIPPING SAUCE

1 cup (30 g) loosely packed fresh mint leaves

1 cup (30 g) loosely packed fresh cilantro leaves

1 green chile, coarsely chopped (optional)

Juice of 1 lime

Salt

To prepare the filling, while the dough is resting, heat the oil in a pan over medium heat. Add the cumin seeds and once they pop, about 1 minute, add the carrots, peas, and kale. Sauté until the carrots are tender, 8–10 minutes. Add the turmeric, garam masala, mint, and cilantro and sauté for 5 minutes longer. Season to taste with salt, and then remove from the heat and let cool for at least 30 minutes.

Preheat the oven to 375°F (190°C) and line a baking sheet with parchment paper.

Divide the dough into 12 equal portions and then roll each one into a ball. On a clean work surface, roll each ball out into a ¼-inch (6-mm)–thick circle using a rolling pin (or a bottle if you don't have a rolling pin). Cut each circle in half and then form a cone with one of the semicircles by folding it in half, aligning the flat sides so that it forms a cone shape. Use a bit of water along the edge to help it stick together. Hold the cone with the pointed end down and the open end up. Use a spoon to fill it about three-quarters of the way up with the filling, making sure to leave enough room to close the samosa. Dab a little water with your finger along the inside edge of the cone's opening and fold the dough over to enclose the filling and to form a triangle. Press the edges firmly together to seal it and, if you'd like a bit more flourish, use a fork to crimp the edges. Continue this process until all of the samosas are ready.

Arrange the samosas on the prepared baking sheet and bake until golden brown, 20–25 minutes.

To prepare the dipping sauce, while the samosas bake, place all of the dipping sauce ingredients in a food processor or blender and purée until smooth. Serve the samosas on a communal platter alongside the dipping sauce. They will keep in a covered container in the refrigerator for up to 3 days.

BOLA BOLA IKAN BALADO

INDONESIA

Vegan Fish Balls

SERVES 4

In Indonesia, bola bola ikan balado is a popular street food that traditionally features fried fish balls tossed in balado sauce, a condiment ubiquitous throughout the country. The version of this dish that is typically enjoyed by monks at Indonesian temples is prepared using vegan fish balls featuring chickpeas and tofu. Even though their version does not contain onions, garlic, or ginger, it retains its vibrancy and depth of flavor. Buddhist monks in Indonesia appreciate this dish not only for its nutritional value—especially the protein power of the tofu and chickpeas—and versatility, but also for its uplifting colors and nuanced flavor profile. The history of bola bola ikan balado is deeply entwined with the vibrant street food culture of Indonesia, a testament to the country's culinary creativity and innovation.

FOR THE VEGAN FISH BALLS

1 package (14 oz/400 g) medium-firm tofu

1 can (14 oz/400 g) chickpeas, drained and rinsed, liquid reserved for the sauce

1½ tablespoons low-sodium soy sauce

1 tablespoon white miso paste

½ cup (10 g) crushed nori flakes

2 tablespoons cornstarch

Preheat the oven to 400°F (200°C). Line a baking sheet with parchment paper or a silicone baking mat.

To prepare the vegan fish balls, in a food processor, combine the tofu, chickpeas, soy sauce, white miso paste, and nori and blend until smooth, pulsing at first to bring everything together. Add the cornstarch and pulse until incorporated. The mixture should be firm enough to form into balls that hold their shape. Shape into balls that are approximately the size of a walnut. Arrange the balls on the prepared baking sheet and bake until the balls are firm and golden brown, about 20 minutes.

Recipe continues

FOR THE BALADO SAUCE

2 tablespoons vegetable oil

8 Roma tomatoes, coarsely chopped

1 large carrot, thinly sliced

1 rib celery, thinly sliced

3 baby bok choy, green and white parts, coarsely shopped

1 red bell pepper, seeded and coarsely chopped

1½ tablespoons low-sodium soy sauce

Reserved chickpea liquid (from the fish balls, see page 163)

2 cups (480 ml) low-sodium vegetable broth

2 tablespoons dark brown sugar

Salt and freshly ground black pepper

Juice of 1 lime

½ cup (15 g) coarsely chopped fresh parsley leaves

Cooked rice, for serving (optional)

Meanwhile, to prepare the balado sauce, heat the oil in a pan over medium heat. Add the tomatoes, carrot, celery, bok choy, and bell pepper and sauté until the tomatoes begin to break down and the other vegetables are just tender, about 5 minutes. Stir in the soy sauce, reserved chickpea liquid, vegetable broth, and dark brown sugar and let simmer until the sauce has thickened, stirring occasionally, 10–15 minutes. Season to taste with salt and pepper. Remove from the heat. Once the vegan fish balls are ready, gently stir them into the sauce along with the lime juice and parsley. Serve in warm bowls with rice, if desired. They will keep in a covered container in the refrigerator for up to 3 days.

BALANCE & SIMPLICITY

At the heart of monastic temple cuisine, the act of growing, preparing, and eating food is approached in the spirit of achieving balance and simplicity. Monks believe that deliberately striving for these two golden principles contributes to a calmer mind that in turn results in a more fulfilling spiritual journey.

Their reverence for a balanced and streamlined existence extends to the principles of minimalist dining rituals that eschew flourishes in favor of a more harmonious and well-rounded experience. Food preparation at the monasteries is an artful exercise in simply composed dishes that shine more for what they don't contain than for unnecessary excess that can weigh us down, both literally and figuratively. Monks skillfully craft dishes with basic and natural ingredients, allowing the true flavors to be illuminated. The emphasis is on nourishment and sustenance rather than elaborate presentations, reflecting their detachment from material desires.

Monastic meals are not just about eating; they are also a spiritual practice—a mindful and communal experience enhanced by a state of equilibrium or stability achieved by distributing elements in such a way that no part becomes overpowering or dominates the other. This intentional awareness creates harmony and avoids excessive or unequal concentration in any particular aspect.

The setting of the table at a temple is intentional and deliberate, with each element symbolizing gratitude, interconnectedness, and a sense of proportion and moderation. As the monks dine together in silence, they savor each bite with full awareness, cultivating a sense of balance with the food they consume, inviting the transference of its simplicity and grace into their minds and spirits.

Science supports the importance of balance and simplicity in our lives, in the context of both food and our daily rituals. A balanced diet that incorporates a variety of nutrients is essential for our physical health, while simplicity in food preparation can reduce stress, retain the integrity of the ingredients we're consuming, and encourage mindful eating.

The practice of balance and simplicity extends beyond the dining table—it positively influences our environment, our relationships, and our daily lives. Simplifying our surroundings and decluttering the table where we gather can create a sense of peace and clarity, fostering a more joyful, hopeful, and optimistic mindset. It can ultimately make us feel more resilient in dealing with the stress we encounter every day. By cultivating a sense of balance in our food choices and simplifying our environment, we regain a sense of control and agency in our lives.

Buddhist monks' agricultural practices also revolve around the key principles of farming and eating in a simple and balanced way. They maintain a harmonious relationship with the land, promoting sustainable agricultural methods and fostering gratitude for the resources provided by nature.

Following the example of achieving balance and simplicity in Buddhist temple cuisine fosters a profound connection with our food and the world around us. It enables us to tap into the wisdom of balance and simplicity in order to infuse our lives with serenity and harmony. Achieving balance and simplicity in our kitchens and at the dining table opens the door to savoring each meal with gratitude and awareness—a celebration of the sacred art of temple cuisine in all its simplicity and grace.

Vegetable Spring Rolls

SERVES 6

Vegetarian spring rolls, or num paen chay as they're called in Cambodia, are a delightful embodiment of Buddhist philosophy. They reflect the principles of balance and simplicity, being neither too rich nor too plain, melding their fresh flavors in a way that is bright and vibrant yet not overpowering, and containing a variety of textures and colors in one delicate, festive package.

Spring rolls are often made in large batches and shared among the community— another echo of the Buddhist values of generosity and interconnectedness. They also serve as a testament to the power of mindful eating, reminding us to savor each bite and appreciate the effort that went into their creation. These vegetarian spring rolls are not just a treat for the palate, but also a symbol of Cambodia's rich cultural and spiritual heritage.

FOR THE SPRING ROLLS

12 spring roll wrappers

½ small head iceberg lettuce, shredded

2 carrots, shredded

1 cucumber, julienned

1½ cups (60 g) bean sprouts

½ cup (15 g) loosely packed fresh mint leaves

½ cup (15 g) loosely packed fresh cilantro leaves

Sesame oil, for serving

Rice vinegar, for serving

Toasted white sesame seeds, for garnish

To prepare the spring rolls, fill a large, shallow dish with warm water. Submerge a spring roll wrapper in the water until it softens, 15–20 seconds. Remove and lay flat on a clean work surface. Place a small amount of each ingredient on the wrapper: lettuce, carrots, cucumber, bean sprouts, a few mint leaves, and cilantro. Roll the wrapper over the ingredients once, fold in the sides, and then continue to roll until sealed. The wrapper should stick to itself and stay closed. Repeat with the remaining wrappers and filling. Once all the spring rolls are assembled, lightly brush them using a pastry brush with a mixture of sesame oil and rice vinegar. This will give them a light sheen and a hint of flavor. Garnish the spring rolls with sesame seeds and serve alongside the peanut sauce for dipping. Spring rolls are best enjoyed fresh but they will keep for up to 1 day in a covered container in the refrigerator.

Recipe continues

FOR THE PEANUT SAUCE

¼ cup (70 g) smooth, low-sodium, sugar-free peanut butter

2 tablespoons low-sodium soy sauce

2 tablespoons warm water

1 tablespoon rice vinegar

1 tablespoon toasted sesame oil

1 tablespoon sugar

To prepare the peanut sauce, combine the peanut butter, soy sauce, water, rice vinegar, sesame oil, and sugar in a small bowl. Whisk until smooth and the sugar is dissolved, then set aside at room temperature.

More Num Paen Chay Ideas

Mango and Avocado
Pair with crisp lettuce and cucumber.

Roasted Sweet Potato and Fresh Cilantro
Accompany with crunchy julienned carrots.

Smoky Tempeh and Apple
Complement with a leafy green, like spinach.

Roasted Red Pepper and Sautéed Zucchini
Bundle with fresh lettuce.

Roasted Butternut Squash and Fresh Sage
Serve with crisp, julienned bell peppers.

Maple-Roasted Carrots and Parsley
Try adding crunchy bean sprouts.

Peanut Tofu and Spinach
Tofu cubes marinated in peanut sauce and then baked, wrapped in fresh spinach leaves.

Jackfruit and Slaw
Tender, pulled jackfruit with a tangy cabbage and carrot slaw.

Grated Raw Beet and Fresh Mint
Complement with julienned cucumber.

Grilled Portobello and Basil
Pair with a tangy pickled carrot and radish mix.

Lemongrass Tempeh and Radish
Tempeh marinated in lemongrass and ginger, combined with thinly sliced radishes and lettuce.

Roasted Brussels Sprouts and Apple
Bundle with fresh spinach.

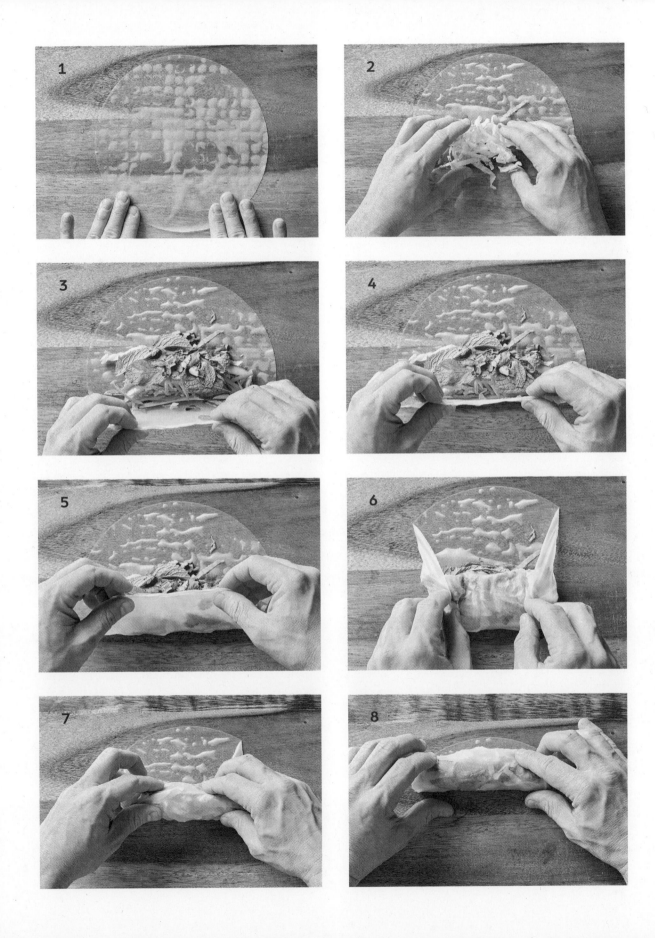

Wat Ounalom Temple
Cambodia

Perched along the eastern riverfront of Cambodia's bustling capital, Phnom Penh, Wat Ounalom, an emblem of resilience and peace, has stood as a reassuring symbol of hope and endurance since the 15th century CE. This tranquil sanctuary is the epicenter of Cambodian Theravada Buddhism, and it has played a pivotal role in maintaining the Buddhist faith even throughout Cambodia's tumultuous history.

Within the temple's hallowed walls, monks' culinary practices reflect the Buddhist principles of balance and simplicity. Their diet revolves around traditional Cambodian dishes like num banh chok (rice noodles with a light vegetable curry), which reflects the principles of equilibrium and the significance of plant-based foods. Eating is enjoyed by the temple monks in silence, underscoring the sanctity of nourishment and being present during meals as opposed to mindlessly eating as we often do in our busy and distracted lives.

The temple, with its golden spires and peaceful aura, is a place of contemplation and learning, serving food to visitors as a reflection of the Buddhist teachings of generosity and kindness. The monks, living embodiments of Buddhist virtues, play an integral part in the Cambodian community, often providing counsel and solace to the community during times of upheaval or turbulence.

Wat Ounalom stands as testament to the power of faith, solidarity, endurance, and community in overcoming adversity, reflecting the indomitable spirit of the Cambodian people amid a tumultuous history.

Clear Dumplings Steamed in Banana Leaves

SERVES 2

Bánh bột lọc is a traditional Vietnamese dish that originates from the central region of the country. It's a clear-looking dumpling made with tapioca starch and traditionally filled with shrimp and pork belly. This version uses a vegan shrimp alternative to align with the Buddhist philosophy of non-harm. It's then wrapped in banana leaves and steamed until cooked. Bánh bột lọc holds a special place in Vietnamese cuisine and is often enjoyed during family gatherings and festivals. Its intricate preparation process signifies the care and effort put into making food for loved ones.

---

1 lb (450 g) vegan shrimp

1 cup (240 ml) vegan fish sauce

1 cup (160 g) tapioca starch

¼ cup (40 g) rice flour

½ cup (120 ml) simmering water

2 banana leaves, cut into sixteen 6 × 3-inch (15 × 7.5-cm) segments using sharp kitchen scissors

In a medium bowl, marinate the vegan shrimp in the fish sauce for 30 minutes. While it marinates, whisk together the tapioca starch and rice flour in a large bowl. Add the simmering water in a slow, steady stream while stirring constantly until it comes together into a dough. Using your hands, knead the dough until its surface is smooth and slightly shiny.

To assemble, set up a steamer over a pan of simmering water. Drain the vegan shrimp and arrange the banana leaf segments on a clean work surface. Place a spoonful of dough at the center of each segment, flatten it, and place a small spoonful of shrimp on top. Cover it with another small spoonful of dough, flattening it over the shrimp to firm a cohesive package of dough. Fold the banana leaf around it on all sides to form a rectangular parcel. Repeat with the remaining leaves, dough, and filling. Transfer the parcels to the steamer (you might have to steam them in two batches, depending upon the size of your steamer). Steam until the dough becomes translucent, about 30 minutes. Transfer to a plate and let cool before serving. These do not keep well and should be enjoyed right away.

Additional Notes on Bánh Bột Lọc

BANANA LEAVES

Banana leaves play a significant role in many Southeast Asian cuisines, including Vietnamese. They add a subtle aroma to the food that's wrapped in them and also serve as a natural and sustainable wrapping material. Their use in Vietnamese cuisine is widespread, from wrapping food for steaming or grilling to serving as plates for communal eating. In Buddhist temple cuisine, there's a deep respect for nature and the environment, and banana leaves are a perfect embodiment of this respect. As they are biodegradable and renewable resources, they fit well with the Buddhist philosophy of minimizing harm to living beings and the environment.

Here are some tips for using banana leaves:

Cleaning
Rinse clean the banana leaves before using them. Use a damp cloth to wipe both sides of the leaf.

Cutting
Cut the leaves into the desired size before you start wrapping. It's easier to cut them while they're still dry and stiff.

Softening
Banana leaves can be a bit stiff. To make them more pliable and easier to fold, quickly pass them over an open flame or dip them in boiling water. The heat makes the leaves softer and releases their natural oils, enhancing the flavor of the wrapped food.

Storage
If you have any leftover leaves, you can store them in the freezer. They will retain their flexibility and freshness when thawed.

TAPIOCA

Tapioca, derived from the cassava root, is widely used in Vietnamese cooking, especially in desserts and snack items like bánh bột lọc. When cooked, it has a unique chewy texture and turns translucent, which is a signature characteristic of many Vietnamese dishes. It is also gluten-free, making it an excellent option for those with dietary restrictions. Like banana leaves, it can be easily sourced at Asian specialty markets. This recipe includes the use of a steamer. If you don't own a steamer, you can follow the instructions for using a homemade steamer on page 130.

Fruit Salad

SERVES 4

Thai watermelon salad is a refreshing dish that embodies the Buddhist principles of balance and simplicity. The balance of sweet and tangy fruits with a subtly spiced dressing creates a harmonious flavor profile, reflecting the Buddhist pursuit of harmony in life. The recipe's simplicity underscores the practice of living a simple life unburdened by unnecessary attachments. Thai Buddhist monks find the dish appealing because it perfectly aligns with these principles while being wholesome and nutritious and celebrates the dizzying array of thirst-quenching fruit available to them in Thailand.

Fruit is a cornerstone in Thai cuisine, prized for its diverse flavors and health benefits, and it plays a pivotal role in creating vibrant salads like this one. Enjoy this invigorating recipe as a dessert, snack, or refreshing side. The cooling fruit flavors, combined with the tangy and creamy dressing, make for a salad that's truly an ode to the Thai appreciation for balance and simplicity in food and in life.

---

4 cups (560 g) cubed watermelon

2 cups (310 g) cubed pineapple

1 cup (170 g) cubed jackfruit (see preparation method for fresh jackfruit on page 107 or use 6 oz/170 g precut jackfruit from a can)

½ cup (120 ml) coconut milk

Zest and juice of 2 limes

2 tablespoons tamarind paste

½ teaspoon crunchy sea salt

Fresh mint leaves, for garnish

In a large bowl, gently toss together the watermelon, pineapple, and jackfruit. In a separate bowl, whisk together the coconut milk, lime zest, lime juice, and tamarind paste until well combined. Drizzle the dressing over the fruit mixture, sprinkle with the sea salt, and gently stir to ensure all the fruit is coated. Chill in the refrigerator for at least 1 hour before serving to let the flavors meld. Garnish with fresh mint leaves just before serving. This salad does not hold up well—the fruit will begin to break down due to the macerating effect of the dressing—and is best enjoyed right away.

Buddhist Symbols

Symbols have always held a potent space in spiritual practices throughout the world, and in Buddhism, they provide a visual language that expresses profound lessons, traditions, and teachings. Symbols serve as reminders of the path to enlightenment, the spiritual journey every Buddhist strives to undertake.

One of the most recognizable symbols is the lotus, representing optimism, purity, and spiritual awakening, often depicted in Buddhist temple architecture, scriptures, and ritual items. Its ability to blossom in murky waters serves as a metaphor for the human condition, rising above the material world toward spiritual enlightenment. In culinary traditions, the lotus root and seeds are common ingredients, symbolizing a path of purity and enlightenment in every bite.

The dharma wheel, another vital symbol, signifies the Buddha's teachings and the path to liberation. Its eight spokes correspond to the Noble Eightfold Path. This emphasis on circularity and cyclicity often extends to the dining rituals in temples, where monks eat mindfully in a circle, embodying the wheel's representation of unity and completeness.

The endless knot, symbolizing the interconnect-edness of all things, echoes the Buddhist principle of dependent origination, suggesting the interconnectedness of all life. This symbol resonates in communal eating experiences, strengthening the bond between individuals and their shared spiritual journey.

These symbols serve as visual reminders of Buddhist philosophies, enriching the path of monks and devotees alike, and rooting their daily rituals and routines, including culinary traditions, in hopeful and profound spiritual meaning.

Lentil Soup

DAL SHORBA

INDIA

SERVES 4

Dal soup, a staple dish in India, embodies the Buddhist principles of balance and simplicity with its minimal yet nourishing ingredients. Dal, or lentils, provide the backbone of Indian cuisine due to their affordability, versatility, and nutritional value. They are packed with protein, fiber, and complex carbohydrates, making them a significant source of energy for the predominantly vegetarian population. This dal soup, bereft of ginger, onions, and garlic, aligns with many Buddhist dietary practices, making it favored among Indian Buddhist monks. Enjoy this soothing and nutritious dish with a side of rice or bread. Its simplicity and balanced flavors make it a perfect example of Indian culinary philosophy, highlighting the principle that nourishment need not be complex to be comforting, warming, and deeply satisfying.

1 cup (200 g) dal (red or brown lentils)

6 cups (1.4 L) water

1 cinnamon stick (optional)

1 teaspoon ground turmeric

1 tablespoon vegetable oil

1 teaspoon cumin seeds

1 Thai red chile, thinly sliced

1 large beefsteak tomato, coarsely chopped

1 teaspoon ground coriander

Salt

Cooked rice, for serving

Naan or roti, for serving (optional)

Rinse the lentils under cold running water until the water runs clear to remove any excess debris.

In a large pot, bring the water to a boil over high heat. Reduce the heat to medium-low and add the lentils, cinnamon stick, if desired, and turmeric. Partially cover the pot and simmer until the lentils are tender, about 30 minutes. If scum forms on the surface of the water during this step, remove it with a spoon.

In a pan, heat the oil over medium heat. Add the cumin seeds and once they begin to crackle, about 1 minute, add the chile and tomato. Sauté until the tomato has broken down, about 10 minutes. Stir in the coriander and cook for 1 minute longer. Stir this into the lentils after they have cooked for 30 minutes and let simmer for 10 minutes longer to enable the flavors to meld. Remove the cinnamon stick and season to taste with salt. Spoon the soup into warm bowls and serve with rice and naan, if desired. The soup will keep in a covered container in the refrigerator for up to 4 days.

Temple Dining
A Spiritual and Culinary Journey

Visiting a monastic temple transcends a mere touristic experience; it offers a deep dive into a culture steeped in spirituality, history, and rich culinary heritage. One of the most intimate ways to connect with this ethos is by partaking in a meal at the temple. Often set in tranquil surroundings, temple meals reflect the spiritual principles of simplicity, mindfulness, gratitude, and compassion.

Most meals served are vegetarian or vegan, in line with the monastic values of sustainability, non-harm, and reverence for all life. Ingredients are fresh, seasonal, and often grown within temple grounds, emphasizing a harmonious relationship with nature. Dishes are often prepared with minimal aromatic foods and spices, allowing the natural flavors of the ingredients to shine. This simplicity is a conscious practice, reminding diners of the importance of reverence and contentment.

Eating at a temple is not just about the food; it's also a meditative experience. Visitors might notice the absence of loud chatter or unnecessary noise. Meals are often consumed in silence, promoting mindfulness in every bite, every flavor and texture. Reflective of the monks who live at the temple, it becomes a practice of being present in the moment. For visitors, dining at a temple can be a transformative, life-changing experience. It offers an illuminating alchemy of spiritual reflection and culinary transcendence, revealing that the nourishment of the body, heart, and spirit can indeed be one and the same.

HONG CAI TOU SHA LA

SINGAPORE

Red Beet Salad

SERVES 4

Chinese cuisine, underpinned by the principles of yin and yang, seeks a harmonious balance in flavors, textures, and colors. This shredded beet salad elegantly encapsulates a symbiotic approach to food presentation and consumption. Hong cai tou sha la originated in China and like so many other iconic Chinese dishes, journeyed across the sea to claim a spot in Singapore's diverse food tapestry. Carried by Chinese immigrants in search of better prospects, this dish, with its bold jewel-toned hue, embodies their resilience, nostalgia, and courage. In the dynamic neighborhoods of Singapore, it melded with local flavors and influences, becoming a testament to the island nation's rich cultural confluence and shared gastronomic heritage.

Beets, with their vibrant ruby red color and subtly sweet flavor, are nutritional powerhouses. They are rich in antioxidants, fiber, and essential vitamins and minerals, beneficial for cardiovascular health and overall wellness. These benefits align with the Buddhist monks' pursuit of nourishment through a plant-based diet that supports both physical and spiritual health. As verse 48 in the *Tao Te Ching* says, "In the pursuit of learning, every day something is acquired. In the pursuit of the Tao, every day something is dropped."

---

2 large red beets (reserve their greens for another use)

1 tablespoon black sesame seeds

1 tablespoon white sesame seeds

3 tablespoons rice vinegar

2 tablespoons toasted sesame oil

1 tablespoon low-sodium soy sauce

1 tablespoon maple syrup or agave

Salt and freshly ground black pepper

Wearing gloves to avoid staining your hands, peel the beets using a vegetable peeler. Either hand-shred the beets on a cheese grater or use a food processor. Transfer to a large bowl. In a dry pan over medium heat, toast the sesame seeds while shaking the pan continuously to prevent burning, until they begin to pop, about 2 minutes.

In a bowl, whisk together the vinegar, oil, soy sauce, and maple syrup until incorporated. Pour over the beets, sprinkle with the toasted sesame seeds, and stir gently until the beets are glistening. Let the salad rest at room temperature for 30 minutes to enable the flavors to meld. Season to taste with salt and pepper and serve. The beet salad will keep in a covered container in the refrigerator for up to 3 days.

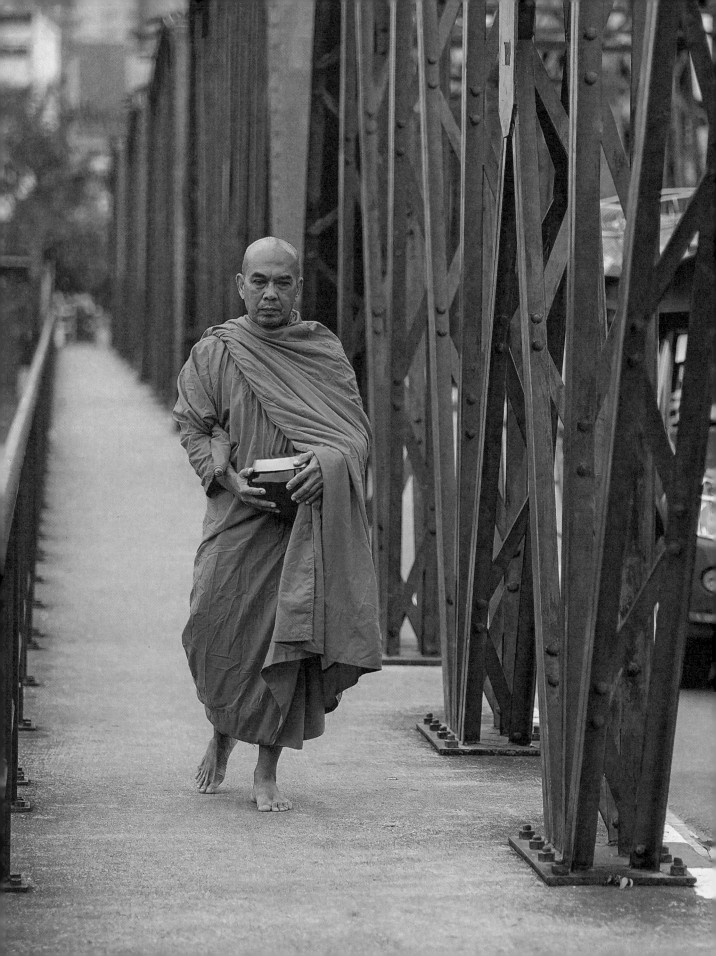

Buddhism and the Modern World

In our fast-paced, digital, and oftentimes distracted society, the time-tested wisdom of Buddhism seems more relevant and important than ever. The fundamental principles of Buddhism—mindfulness, compassion, gratitude, balance, and the pursuit of inner peace—offer valuable guidance in navigating the complexities of our modern world.

Mindfulness, a core teaching of Buddhism, promotes a fully engaged and conscious state of living regardless of the contemporary world's noisy distractions. With the current trend of multitasking and the constant influx of digital information, this practice encourages us to slow down, fostering mental clarity and reducing stress. Many corporations and institutions now incorporate mindfulness into their work culture, recognizing its benefits on productivity, happiness, and overall well-being.

The principle of compassion in Buddhism, extending not just to others but also to oneself and to the planet and all of its living beings, offers a counterpoint to the consumerism, consumption, self-criticism, and comparison often triggered by social media. It fosters the quiet reassurance of empathy and interconnectedness in our global society, underpinning movements toward social justice, environmental sustainability, and animal rights.

Buddhism's emphasis on the impermanence of all things provides a valuable perspective amid the rapid changes, anxiety, and uncertainties of our time. It helps individuals cultivate resilience and adaptability, equipping them to handle life's ups and downs with grace and equanimity.

Buddhism's timeless wisdom can serve as a compass in the modern world, guiding us toward a more mindful, compassionate, and balanced way of living.

Vegetable Sandwich

SERVES 4

Bánh mì, a vibrant sandwich that marries the culinary traditions of Vietnam and France, is a time-honored masterpiece of diverse flavors, colors, and textures. The term *bánh mì* refers to bread in Vietnamese, specifically a baguette, a nod to the French influence during the colonial period. Over the years, this sandwich has evolved into a unique Vietnamese dish, with a wide array of fillings ranging from grilled meat to colorful fresh and pickled vegetables.

Among vegetarian versions of bánh mì, bánh mì chay holds a special place in Vietnamese hearts, and it is also beloved by Vietnamese Buddhist monks. Bánh mì chay, with its colorful medley of vegetables and plant-based proteins like tempeh, reflects this ethos in a sandwich that is as appetizing as it is nutritious, since it is packed with herbs, vegetables, and other health-boosting ingredients. Don't forget to top your sandwiches with a generous handful of fresh cilantro and a spread like vegan mayo or hummus. The act of preparing and eating this sandwich can be seen as a practice in mindfulness, savoring the varied flavors, colors, and textures and feeling grateful for their journey from the earth to the table.

PICKLED VEGETABLES

1 cup (240 ml) rice vinegar

1 cup (240 ml) water

2 tablespoons sugar

1 tablespoon kosher salt

1 large carrot, julienned

6 red radishes, thinly sliced

TEMPEH

2 tablespoons soy sauce

1 tablespoon mirin

1 tablespoon toasted sesame oil

1 teaspoon sugar

¾ lb (340 g) tempeh, sliced into 12 portions

To prepare the pickled vegetables, combine the vinegar, water, sugar, and salt in a pot over medium heat and whisk until the sugar dissolves. Remove from the heat and add the carrot and radishes. Set aside until cooled. Drain.

To prepare the tempeh, combine the soy sauce, mirin, sesame oil, and sugar in a large bowl and whisk until the sugar dissolves. Add the tempeh slices and marinate for 30 minutes. Drain. Heat a pan over medium heat and fry the tempeh until golden brown on both sides, about 3 minutes per side, drizzling with the marinade to allow the tempeh to absorb as much flavor as possible.

Recipe continues

FOR ASSEMBLY

Vegan mayonnaise

4 small baguettes, sliced
and toasted

1½ cups (135 g) shredded
napa cabbage

½ cup (15 g) loosely packed
fresh cilantro leaves

To assemble the sandwiches, slather the mayonnaise on both interior portions of the baguettes. Arrange the tempeh inside and top with the shredded cabbage, pickled vegetables, and cilantro. Serve right away. The bánh mì is best enjoyed immediately but it will keep in a covered container in the refrigerator for up to 1 day (although it will become soggy).

More Bánh Mì Ideas

Lemongrass Tempeh
Tempeh marinated in a lemongrass and ginger sauce, then sautéed. Serve with pickled radishes and carrots.

Maple Miso Tofu
Tofu marinated in maple syrup and miso sauce, then baked until crispy. Include pickled daikon radish (see page 150) and cucumber.

Soy Ginger Mushrooms
A mix of mushrooms sautéed in soy sauce and ginger. Pair with a pickled salad of beets and carrots.

Roasted Sweet Potato
Sweet potato slices roasted with olive oil, salt, and smoked paprika. Add a tangy slaw of pickled cabbage (see page 140).

Lentil Patties
Patties made from cooked lentils, bread crumbs, and herbs. Serve with a pickled medley of carrot, radish, and cucumber.

Jackfruit "Pulled Pork"
Jackfruit simmered in a tamari and maple syrup mixture until it can be shredded. Include pickled jicama for crunch.

Roasted Butternut Squash
Squash roasted with olive oil, cumin, and coriander until tender. Add a pickled apple and carrot slaw for a sweet contrast.

Teriyaki Seitan
Seitan slices marinated in a homemade teriyaki sauce (soy sauce, mirin, sugar, and ginger), then pan-fried. Serve with pickled cucumber and radishes.

BBQ Cauliflower
Cauliflower florets tossed in barbecue sauce and roasted until tender. Pair with pickled red cabbage.

Peanut Tempeh
Tempeh marinated in a peanut sauce (made from peanut butter, soy sauce, and agave), then pan-fried. Include a tangy pickled cucumber salad.

Roasted Chickpeas
Chickpeas roasted with tamari and maple syrup until crispy. Add a slaw of pickled carrots and daikon.

Vegan "Egg" Salad
Mashed tofu mixed with vegan mayo, turmeric, and black salt for an egg-like flavor. Serve with pickled beets.

Sesame Peanut Noodles

SERVES 4

This recipe, in its essence, exemplifies the Buddhist ideals of equilibrium and minimalism. The combination of humble ingredients brings a harmony of flavors and textures—from the earthy and slightly nutty soba noodles to the tangy, silken peanut sauce to the freshness of spinach and the light crunch of the sesame seeds.

1 package (12 oz/340 g) buckwheat noodles, such as soba

3 cups (90 g) loosely packed fresh baby spinach

1½ tablespoons toasted sesame oil

1 lemongrass stalk, tough outer leaves removed and interior thinly sliced

½ cup (140 g) smooth, low-sodium peanut butter

1 tablespoon low-sodium soy sauce

1 tablespoon rice vinegar

1 tablespoon vegan fish sauce

1 tablespoon agave or maple syrup

White sesame seeds, for garnish

Cook the soba noodles according to the package instructions. Reserve ⅔ cup (160 ml) of the cooking liquid and then drain the noodles. Rinse them under cold running water to stop the cooking process.

While the noodles are cooking, prepare an ice bath and bring a pot of water to a simmer. Blanch the spinach leaves by adding them to the simmering water and then removing them using a slotted spoon or a spider after 1 minute. Transfer to the ice bath to stop the blanching process. This step will keep the leaves a vibrant green throughout the rest of the recipe preparation.

Heat the oil in a saucepan over medium heat. Add the lemongrass and sauté until it is tender and aromatic, about 3 minutes. Reduce the heat to low and add the peanut butter. Stir until it is loose and smooth, about 2 minutes. Stir in the reserved noodle cooking liquid, soy sauce, rice vinegar, fish sauce, and agave and cook until the sauce has slightly thickened, about 7 minutes. While the sauce is cooking, remove the spinach from the ice bath using a slotted spoon and squeeze excess liquid from it. Add the spinach to the sauce and stir until it has warmed through, about 1 minute. Add the noodles and gently stir until they are uniformly coated in the sauce. Transfer to warm plates and garnish with sesame seeds. Serve while warm. The noodles will keep in a covered container in the refrigerator for up to 3 days.

MINDFULNESS, RESPECT & GRATITUDE

Mindfulness, respect, and gratitude are essential values deeply ingrained in monastic temple cuisine and the daily lives of the monks who hone their spiritual practices there. These principles infuse every aspect of food-growing practices, preparation, and consumption, fostering enriching nourishment for the body but also a deeper connection with our spirits, one another, our communities, and the planet too.

The Buddha eloquently emphasized the importance of mindfulness, respect, and gratitude in temple cuisine and Buddhism, stating, "Let us rise up and be thankful, for if we didn't learn a lot today, at least we learned a little, and if we didn't learn a little, at least we didn't get sick, and if we got sick, at least we didn't die; so, let us all be thankful."

At the monasteries, mindfulness begins with the cultivation of food. Monks approach food-growing practices and gardening with a sense of reverence for the land and the resources it provides. Sustainable agricultural methods are employed, and each stage of cultivation is approached with mindfulness and care.

Temple food preparation is a revered and sacred art, where gratitude guides every step. The process of gathering ingredients, washing, chopping, and cooking is executed with acute awareness, infusing every dish with intention and appreciation. As the monks set the table, they do so with respect for the nourishment their meal provides and for the interconnectedness with all living beings.

Monks practice gratitude in order to recognize the efforts that went into the cultivation and preparation of their food. This fosters a sense of connection with the sustenance they receive and the people who grew and prepared it. It reminds them to be appreciative of the abundance in their lives, which they do not measure against material wealth. Abundance springs instead from sitting down at the table in the company of a supportive community to enjoy a simple, healthful meal.

Science backs the importance of practicing gratitude, which can lead to improved mental health, increased happiness, and reduced stress. When we thoughtfully nurture gratitude, our brains release neurotransmitters that promote positive emotions and well-being, resulting in lasting, transformative benefits.

Considerately approaching each meal with respect and intention enhances our ability to be fully present and engaged in the moment. Reducing how much our minds wander when we eat and maintaining focus reduces stress and promotes mental clarity. Valuing the resources that sustain us fosters a deeper connection with our environment and the world around us.

Incorporating mindfulness, respect, and gratitude into our daily routines can be as simple as taking a few moments each day to reflect on the things we are grateful for. By developing a mindfulness practice, we can experience moments of peace and tranquility amid the chaos of our modern world, empowering us to take action and navigate daily challenges with resilience and optimism.

At the monasteries, gratitude and respect are not limited to the food but extend to every aspect of life. Monks practice gratitude for the opportunity to be of service, to learn, to care for one another with grace and dignity, and to flourish on their spiritual journey. This deep sense of appreciation and interconnectedness with all beings and for the sacred light that burns within each one of us ignites an atmosphere of harmony and unity in our physical world and in our minds, bodies, and spirits too.

Coconut Soup

SERVES 4

Laksa, a comforting blend of bright aromatics, healthful spices, hearty noodles, and creamy coconut milk, tells a captivating tale of migration, culture, and culinary evolution in a fortifying bowl of velvety soup. Believed to have Chinese and Malay roots, this sumptuous noodle soup embodies Southeast Asia's vibrant food landscape. As trade and communities flourished, laksa migrated from its birthplace to ports like Singapore, where it became deeply embedded in the local cuisine. The rich coconut broth, fragranced with lemongrass, offers solace for the spirit, making it a beloved dish for Buddhist monks in Singapore's temples. These temples, aside from being spiritual havens, have become culinary destinations. Visitors seek not only blessings and a cleansing meditative retreat from the chaotic world but also the opportunity to savor this reassuring laksa, a dish that illuminates the principles of compassion, non–harm, and hospitality.

---

2 lemongrass stalks, tough outer leaves removed and tender interior thinly sliced

1 teaspoon ground coriander

1 teaspoon ground turmeric

1 tablespoon vegetable oil

6 cups (1.4 L) low–sodium vegetable broth

1 can (14 oz/400 g) coconut milk

1 tablespoon vegan fish sauce

1 package (8 oz/225 g) rice noodles

1 package (6 oz/170 g) soft tofu, cut into bite–size pieces

Juice of 1 lemon

1 cup (40 g) bean sprouts

Fresh cilantro leaves, for garnish

Lime wedges, for serving

Prepare the spice paste by blending together 2 tablespoons of the lemongrass, coriander, and turmeric in a spice grinder, food processor, or using a mortar and pestle. Add a little water if necessary to achieve a smooth paste.

In a large pot, heat the oil over medium heat and add the spice paste. Sauté until it is aromatic, about 2 minutes. Add the remaining lemongrass and sauté for 1 minute longer. Add the vegetable broth, coconut milk, and fish sauce and stir to combine. Raise the heat to medium–high and bring to a vigorous simmer. Reduce the heat to medium–low, partially cover, and gently simmer for 20 minutes.

While the laksa simmers, prepare the noodles according to the package instructions. Drain, then rinse the noodles under cold running water to prevent them from sticking together. Add the tofu and lemon juice to the soup and simmer until the tofu is warmed through, about 5 minutes. Distribute the noodles and bean sprouts among warm bowls and then spoon the laksa on top. Garnish with cilantro and serve with lime wedges. The laksa will keep in a covered container in the refrigerator for up to 3 days.

Kong Meng San Phor Kark See Monastery

Singapore

Kong Meng San Phor Kark See Monastery, located in Bishan, Singapore, is a beacon of Buddhist spirituality. Rooted in a culinary tradition that emphasizes vegetarianism, dishes prepared here, like the popular laksa (see page 199), a noodle soup that often includes coconut milk, reflects the gratitude, mindfulness, and respect that is embraced by Buddhist monks.

As the largest Buddhist monastery in Singapore, Kong Meng San Phor Kark See, also known as the Bright Hill Temple, is a grand architectural masterpiece adorned with intricate carvings and serene gardens that invite monks and visitors alike to wander through as a pathway along their spiritual journey. Founded in 1921, the temple has become an important sanctuary for Buddhist teachings in Singapore. Buddhism, introduced to Singapore relatively recently in the 19th century, is impactful on Singaporeans' daily lives, promoting a peaceful coexistence among diverse ethnic and religious communities.

A unique aspect of the monks' daily routine is the practice of *pindapata*, the collecting of alms, symbolizing humility and interdependence. This practice reinforces their connection beyond the temple walls to the community, whose citizens often provide the ingredients used in temple meals.

The monastery also extends its vegetarian dining experience to visitors, allowing them to participate in the ritual of mindful eating inside the uplifting temple grounds. A meal here is not merely about sustenance but serves as a reminder of the Buddhist principles of gratitude and respect, encouraging a deep appreciation for life's nourishing gifts.

CHANA MASALA
INDIA

Chickpea Stew
SERVES 4

Chana masala, an enduring staple from India, embodies the principles of simplicity, mindfulness, and gratitude that form the bedrock of Buddhist philosophy. The dish, also known as chole masala, is an ode to the versatility and nutritional richness of chickpeas, simmered to perfection in a tangy, spiced sauce.

Preparing chana masala, with its careful balance of spices and slow cooking process, becomes a meditative act, turning the kitchen into a sanctuary of aromas and flavors. Eating the dish allows for a moment of reverence for the journey of each ingredient, from seed to plate, and for the hands that nurtured and prepared them.

---

2 tablespoons vegetable oil

1 tablespoon cumin seeds

1 tablespoon tomato paste

1 onion, finely chopped

3 cloves garlic, minced

1 inch (2.5 cm) piece fresh ginger, peeled and minced

1 cup (200 g) coarsely chopped tomatoes

1 teaspoon garam masala

1 teaspoon ground turmeric

1 teaspoon ground coriander

½ teaspoon red chile powder, such as Kashmiri

2 cans (14 oz/400 g) chickpeas (undrained)

½ cup (120 ml) water

Salt

Fresh cilantro leaves, for garnish

Cooked rice, for serving

Naan or roti, for serving

In a pan, heat the oil over medium heat. Add the cumin seeds and once they begin to sizzle, about 1 minute, add the tomato paste, onion, garlic, and ginger. Sauté until the onion is golden brown, 7–9 minutes. Add the tomatoes, garam masala, turmeric, coriander, and red chile powder and cook until the tomatoes have broken down and are very soft, about 7 minutes.

Add the chickpeas and their liquid and stir until they are completely coated. Add the water, reduce the heat to medium-low, and cook for 10 minutes longer, stirring occasionally. Season to taste with salt. Spoon the chana masala into warm bowls, garnish with cilantro, and serve with rice and naan. The stew will keep in a covered container in the refrigerator for up to 3 days.

Sweet and Tangy Kelp Salad

SERVES 4

Miyeok muchim is a dish that exemplifies the principles of balance and simplicity that are central to Korean Buddhist temple food. It avoids pungent ingredients like garlic, onions, and chiles, emphasizing mild and natural flavors that reflect the tranquility of monastic life.

Kelp, the main ingredient in miyeok muchim, is highly nutritious. It's rich in iodine, which supports thyroid function, and it's also a good source of vitamin K, calcium, and magnesium. Kelp is high in fiber and low in calories, making it a healthy addition to many meals.

¾ lb (340 g) miyeok (dried kelp)

2 tablespoons low-sodium soy sauce

2 tablespoons toasted sesame oil

2 tablespoons rice vinegar

1½ tablespoons mirin

2 tablespoons toasted white sesame seeds, plus sesame seeds for garnish (optional)

1 red chile, thinly sliced (optional)

Soak the dried miyeok in cold water to cover for at least 30 minutes to soften it. Drain and rinse thoroughly under cold running water to remove any slime buildup and excess salt. Cut into bite-size slices, if necessary. In a large bowl, whisk together the soy sauce, sesame oil, rice vinegar, mirin, sesame seeds, and chile, if using, until the dressing is incorporated. Add the kelp and gently stir until it is glistening. Let it rest in the refrigerator to enable the flavors to meld for at least 30 minutes. Serve it chilled, garnished with additional sesame seeds, if desired. The salad will keep in a covered container in the refrigerator for up to 1 day.

Green Curry

SERVES 4

Thai Buddhist monks honor principles of remaining in the moment by cooking and dining in an abiding spirit of gratitude and by mindfully selecting and preparing ingredients for meals, like this green curry. Omitting onion, garlic, and ginger makes it suitable for Buddhist dietary practices or for those with sensitivities. This dish is more than food; it embodies a rich cultural history and is a vegetarian expression of non-harm.

---

2 tablespoons vegetable oil

2 packages (12 oz/340 g) firm tofu, cut into bite-size cubes

¼ cup (60 g) green curry paste

1 can (14 oz/400 g) coconut milk

2 ribs celery, thinly sliced

1 tablespoon low-sodium soy sauce or tamari

1 tablespoon vegan fish sauce

Juice of 2 limes

4 makrut lime leaves, sliced

Broccoli florets from 1 large head broccoli (save the stem for another use)

2 cups (200 g) trimmed and halved green beans

1 cup (30 g) loosely torn and lightly packed fresh Thai basil leaves

4 cups (620 g) cooked brown rice

Line a plate with paper towels. Heat the oil in a wok over medium heat and sauté the tofu until it is golden brown, 6–8 minutes. Drain on the paper towels. Add the curry paste to the wok and sauté for a few minutes until it becomes aromatic. Add the coconut milk and stir until incorporated. Reduce the heat to medium-low and stir in the celery, soy sauce, fish sauce, lime juice, and lime leaves. Gently simmer for 10 minutes, stirring occasionally. Add the broccoli and green beans and cook until the vegetables are tender, about 6 minutes. Stir in the fried tofu and Thai basil leaves and cook for 1 minute longer. Serve with a bowl of brown rice. The curry will keep in a covered container in the refrigerator for up to 4 days.

Meditation, Breath, and Yoga

Meditation, breath control, and yoga are integral components of many spiritual practices, with their roots deeply embedded in the cultivation of presence and bodily awareness. These practices, pivotal in a monk's daily rituals, contribute significantly to their spiritual progress, physical health, and overall well-being.

Meditation in monastic life is often centered around mindfulness—encouraging practitioners to pay careful attention to the present moment. This practice, when applied to eating and cooking, transforms these mundane acts into profound experiences of awareness and appreciation, making every bite or every stir of a spoon a moment of deep connection to the food and its origins.

Breath control, or pranayama, is another key practice. It involves conscious regulation of breath, fostering focus, calm, and the clear perception of reality. In the context of culinary rituals, mindful breathing can help engender a serene, deliberate approach to food preparation and consumption, heightening the sensory experience and imbuing whatever is being prepared with positive, optimistic energy.

Yoga, often seen as a physical discipline, in its traditional context, is a holistic system encompassing ethical disciplines, physical postures, breath control, and meditative practices. The mindful movement of yoga, like in preparing a meal, can become a form of moving meditation, where focus is given to each gesture, promoting a state of flow and cohesiveness.

The Buddha emphasized the importance of mindfulness in all activities. By incorporating these practices into daily life and into our dining and food preparation rituals, not just on the yoga mat or meditation cushion, we cultivate a greater sense of connectedness, reverence for life, gratitude, and ultimately, inner peace.

Mushroom Stew

SERVES 4

Mushroom bhaji is a flavorful, spiced Indian dish often enjoyed as a side or main course, especially in North India. It's a plant-based recipe incorporating a diverse range of vegetables and a medley of spices, providing a nutritious meal embodying the Buddhist principles of mindfulness, respect, and gratitude. Each bite can thus become a conscious act of living in harmony with the world.

2 tablespoons vegetable oil

2 teaspoons cumin seeds

1 large yellow onion, thinly sliced

1 red chile, seeded and thinly sliced

1 inch (2.5 cm) piece fresh ginger, peeled and minced

4 cloves garlic, minced

1 teaspoon ground turmeric

1 teaspoon ground coriander

½ teaspoon red chile powder, such as Kashmiri

1 large beefsteak tomato, coarsely chopped

3 cups (270 g) coarsely chopped mushrooms, such as cremini or white button

1 yellow zucchini, quartered and thinly sliced

1½ cups (360 ml) low-sodium vegetable broth

Salt

Fresh cilantro leaves, for garnish

Hot cooked rice, for serving

Warm naan, for serving (optional)

In a pan, heat the oil over medium heat. Add the cumin seeds and once they start to sizzle, about 1 minute, add the onion, chile, ginger, and garlic and sauté until the onion is a deep golden brown, about 8 minutes. Add the turmeric, coriander, and red chile powder and sauté for a few minutes longer. Add the tomatoes and sauté until they have completely broken down and a thick sauce begins to form, 8–10 minutes. Add the mushrooms and zucchini and sauté for 3 minutes longer.

Add the vegetable broth, reduce the heat to low, partially cover the pan, and cook until a thick stew has formed, stirring occasionally to prevent scorching, about 10 minutes. Season to taste with salt. Spoon into warm bowls and garnish with cilantro. Serve with rice and naan, if desired. The stew will keep in a covered container in the refrigerator for up to 3 days.

NOTE: For a drier version, reduce the amount of vegetable stock to 1 cup (240 ml) or even ¾ cup (180 ml), depending upon your preference.

Alms

The tradition of laypeople offering alms, or donations of food and other useful items, is an important custom in many temple traditions. Also referred to as *dana*, alms are offered to monastics for a number of important reasons that reflect the fundamental principles of Buddhism and other religions. Alms-giving symbolizes the spirit of generosity and altruism that is the beating heart of what it means to be a monk.

Selflessly offering an item of value to another is compassion in action. It encourages a daily practice of giving without personal gain; those who offer alms do not expect a return on their donation. They invest in the well-being of monastics simply because it is the generous thing to do. The offering enables monks and nuns to completely commit to their spiritual practice without concerning themselves with procuring the daily necessities they need to survive.

Alms-giving teaches the important principle of letting go of material possessions to make more room for gratitude and benevolence. The ritual offers the giver an opportunity to accumulate positive karma, which ultimately leads to a more favorable outcome in their future well-being and spiritual growth. It is a virtuous cycle that benefits the giver and receiver in equal measure and is practiced with abiding joy and gratitude.

Shiso Mango Salad

SERVES 4

This salad is a loving nod to Vietnam's fascinating tapestry of culinary traditions, offering a window into the nation's vibrant, flavor-packed, plant-based cuisine that has been shaped by a complex, intriguing, and storied history of resilience, courage, and resourcefulness. It's a delightful mix of textures and tastes, echoing the diversity and harmony of Vietnamese food and culture.

Shiso is available in two varieties (green and purple). Either variety (or a mix of both) will do for this recipe.

FOR THE DRESSING

Juice of 2 limes

2 tablespoons mirin

2 tablespoons low-sodium soy sauce

1½ tablespoons toasted sesame oil

1½ tablespoons agave or maple syrup

1 tablespoon minced, peeled fresh ginger (optional)

FOR THE SALAD

2 large ripe mangoes, peeled, seeded, and thinly sliced

1½ cups (45 g) coarsely torn and loosely packed shiso leaves

1 large carrot, shredded

1½ cups (90 g) shredded iceberg lettuce

1 large cucumber, julienned

⅔ cup (80 g) finely chopped toasted unsalted cashews

Crunchy sea salt, for serving

To prepare the dressing, in a small bowl, whisk together the lime juice, mirin, soy sauce, sesame oil, agave, and ginger, if using, until incorporated.

To prepare the salad, in a large bowl, toss together the mangoes, shiso leaves, carrot, lettuce, cucumber, and cashews. Pour the dressing over the salad and gently toss until everything glistens. Season with crunchy sea salt. Serve immediately. This salad doesn't keep very well because the shiso becomes limp and the mangoes turn a bit slimy, so it's suggested to enjoy it right away!

Shiso

Shiso, also known as perilla, is an intriguing green or purple herb with a complex flavor profile that comes in two varieties and makes frequent appearances in Vietnamese, Japanese, and Korean cuisines. Its unique mosaic of flavors combines notes of mint, basil, and a hint of anise, offering a refreshing and intricate taste to any dish. Shiso makes a frequent appearance in the herb gardens at Buddhist temples in Asia, where it is appreciated for how easy it is to cultivate, its jewel-toned wash of color, and the subtle way it perfumes the air. Shiso highlights the simplicity yet lushness of flavors, colors, and ingredients in Vietnamese cuisine, particularly when paired with the nation's beloved mango, celebrated for its luscious texture and tropical sweetness.

Remember that shiso leaves have a strong flavor, so it's always a good idea to experiment with small amounts until you find the balance that suits your palate. Here are some alternative uses for shiso leaves:

Shiso Pesto
Replace basil with shiso leaves in your traditional pesto recipe for a unique twist. The leaves can be blended with garlic, pine nuts or toasted hazelnuts or pumpkin seeds, plant-based parmesan, and olive oil.

Shiso Tea
You can brew the leaves to make a soothing and aromatic tea. Just steep the leaves in hot water and add a drizzle of agave or maple syrup, if desired.

Shiso Salad Dressing
Blend shiso leaves with olive oil, vinegar, and a spoonful of agave or maple syrup to create a flavorful and refreshing salad dressing.

Pickled Shiso
Pickling shiso leaves in a vinegar-based brine is a great way to preserve them. They can be used to add a tangy, citrusy flavor to various dishes.

Shiso Pasta
Toss a handful of shiso into your favorite pasta recipe. It's the perfect way to perk up its flavor and color profile.

Shiso Soup
Add shiso leaves to miso or clear broth soups for a burst of complex flavor.

Shiso Rice
You can mix finely chopped shiso leaves into cooked rice to add a unique flavor. Shiso pairs particularly well with fish- or vegetable-based dishes.

Shiso Tempura
Lightly battered and deep-fried shiso leaves make a delicious and visually impressive side dish or appetizer.

Shiso Wraps
Shiso leaves can be used as a wrapper for grilled tempeh, tofu, or veggies, similar to lettuce wraps.

Shiso Plant-Based Ice Cream
The leaves can be steeped in plant-based cream (cashew is especially lovely) to create a uniquely flavored homemade ice cream or sorbet. The flavor pairs well with fruits like strawberries and plums.

INDEX

JODY EDDY is a James Beard Award–nominated and IACP Award-winning author of seven cookbooks. Her work has been featured in *The New York Times*, *Vogue*, *The Wall Street Journal*, *The Washington Post*, *The Guardian*, *Gourmet*, *Bon Appétit*, and CNN, among others. She is a graduate of the University of Minnesota and the Institute of Culinary Education in Manhattan, and she has cooked at the Michelin 3-star restaurants Jean-Georges in NYC and Heston Blumenthal's The Fat Duck in England, along with the late chef Floyd Cardoz's Tabla in NYC. Jody is currently writing her first novel. She is based in northern Spain.

WEBSITE: jodyeddy.com

INSTAGRAM: @jodyeddy

SUBSTACK: What's Good Here

NewSeed
PRESS

an imprint of Insight Editions
P.O. Box 3088
San Rafael, CA 94912
www.insighteditions.com

Text © 2024 Jody Eddy

ISBN: 979-8-88674-139-1

ROOTS of PEACE   REPLANTED PAPER

Insight Editions, in association with Roots of
Peace, will plant two trees for each tree used in the
manufacturing of this book. Roots of Peace is an
internationally renowned humanitarian organization
dedicated to eradicating land mines worldwide and
converting war-torn lands into productive farms
and wildlife habitats. Roots of Peace will plant two
million fruit and nut trees in Afghanistan and provide
farmers there with the skills and support necessary
for sustainable land use.

Publisher Raoul Goff

Associate Publisher Roger Shaw

Publishing Director Katie Killebrew

VP, Creative Director Chrissy Kwasnik

VP Manufacturing Alix Nicholaeff

Associate Art Director Megan Sinead Bingham

Production Designer Jean Hwang

Editor Peter Adrian Behravesh

Assistant Editor Amanda Nelson

Sr Production Manager Joshua Smith

Sr Production Manager, Subsidiary Rights
  Lina s Palma-Temena

Photographs on pages 1, 2, 10, 13, 18–19, 23, 27, 31,
32, 40–41, 44, 50, 54, 58, 62–63, 66, 70, 73, 80, 82–83,
87, 90, 94, 100, 108–109, 117, 120, 126, 129, 136–137,
144, 154, 160, 165, 166–167, 170, 173, 179, 182, 187, 191,
194–195, 198, 202, 208, 213, and 222 by Waterbury
Publications, Inc.

Photograph on page 223 courtesy of Kristin Teig.

All photographs not specified above courtesy of
Shutterstock, Inc.

NewSeed would also like to thank Karen Levy, Mary
J. Cassells, and Elizabeth Parson for their work on
this book.

Manufactured in India by Insight Editions

10 9 8 7 6 5 4 3 2 1